200 vege
growing bas

D0331787

200 vegetable-growing basics

growing basics

hamlyn **all color**

Richard Bird

An Hachette UK company
www.hachette.co.uk

First published in Great Britain in 2009 by Hamlyn,
a division of Octopus Publishing Group Ltd
2–4 Heron Quays, London E14 4JP
www.octopusbooksusa.com

Distributed in the U.S. and Canada by Octopus Books USA:
c/o Hachette Book Group
237 Park Avenue
New York NY 10017

ISBN: 978-0-600-62036-5

Printed and bound in China

1 2 3 4 5 6 7 8 9 10

contents

introduction

Anyone who grows their own vegetables will agree that they taste far better than anything you can buy. Commercial growers choose varieties that travel well, are uniform in appearance, and ripen at the same time. Gardeners, however, can choose varieties purely for flavor.

It's not just a question of choosing the best varieties, however—flavor is also about freshness. Many vegetables, including sweet corn and peas, contain sugars that contribute to their wonderful taste. As soon as they are picked, the sugars begin to convert to starch and the flavor deteriorates. This is why supermarket vegetables can't compete with a handful of the sweetest peas picked a few moments before cooking.

Another good reason to grow your own is one of practicality. If you feel like adding a few scallions to a salad you have them to hand. If unexpected visitors arrive you can gather a few extra eggplants for lunch.

If you also take into account the satisfaction you feel, the beneficial exercise, and the fact that you know exactly what has been put on your vegetables, you will soon realize that home-grown is best. All you need to get started is a small area of soil or a few containers on the patio and a little time. This handy book contains more than 200 invaluable hints and tips on growing your own vegetables; in fact, everything you need to know to get growing.

getting started

organic or nonorganic?

Much has been said in the media about what you should or should not eat, and whether organic food is better for your health than nonorganic produce. Similarly, there is also a debate about organic gardening—should you be using chemicals on your vegetable beds and community gardens?

what does organic mean?

Nonorganic gardeners use artificially manufactured, chemical fertilizers, pesticides, and herbicides. Organic gardeners avoid chemicals altogether because of their impact on the environment and on beneficial wildlife, although some may resort to pesticides derived from plants and other natural ingredients.

developing the right philosophy

To a good gardener, however, organic versus nonorganic need not become an issue. Making and using your own compost is not a question of belief but one of good gardening practice. In addition, having a mixture of flowers as well as vegetables is largely a matter of common sense (see page 24). Beneficial insects as well as pests are attracted to the garden, and there is a balance that rarely needs interference. By practicing good husbandry (see page 40), you shouldn't need to use any treatments to keep pests at bay. And if a problem does arise, you can simply remove the crop and discard it, then have another go next year. This is one great advantage that growing vegetables has over other more permanent plants, such as trees and shrubs.

soil

Soil is the very stuff of gardening. Get it right and you stand a good chance of producing a fine array of vegetables. You may have an old garden that has near-perfect soil or you may have a new garden still full of construction debris. No matter what your starting point, a little effort is all it will take.

the ideal soil

The ideal soil is fertile and free draining yet moisture retentive. The last two terms may seem to contradict one another, but what they mean is that a soil retains enough water for the plants to thrive but does not become waterlogged in wet weather.

amending the texture

The soil in new gardens built over solid clay is among the worst you may encounter. However, after carefully cultivating the soil for even as little as two years, you can transform it into something quite respectable. The key is to add plenty of well-rotted organic material (humus) in the form of compost, animal manure, or commercial soil amendments. Any of these will help to break down the soil and encourage worms, which will amend it even further.

Grit or fine gravel is also invaluable for improving the drainage and soil texture. Dig some into the soil at the same time as the organic matter. For more details on soil preparation see page 22.

amending the fertility

As well as amending soil texture, well-rotted organic material will also provide nutrients to fertilize the plants. Add plenty of well-rotted organic material, such as compost or animal manure, to the soil when you are digging it at the end of the fall, so that it has a chance to break down before sowing and planting in spring. Some plants—parsnips for example—do not like newly fertilized ground, so plant these crops in areas that have been treated the previous year. Mention is made under individual plants when this is required.

With permanent crops, such as asparagus, apply a layer of well-rotted compost or manure around the plants at the beginning of each season. There is no need to dig it in—the worms will take it into the soil for you.

Other fertilizers, such as bonemeal or all-purpose fertilizer, can be used to give a boost to soil fertility. Sprinkle them on the surface of the soil and rake in before planting. If there are already plants growing in the soil, sprinkle the fertilizer on the soil surface and water in. Always apply at the rate recommended on the package.

soil pH

On the whole, vegetables are a tolerant lot, but the acidity or alkalinity of the soil can be important. Generally speaking, vegetables prefer a neutral soil—that is, a pH of 7—but some crops, such as brassicas, prefer a slightly alkaline soil. To check the pH (the measure of acidity/alkalinity) of your soil, buy a soil-testing kit at a garden center. They are simple to use and will tell you the pH value of your soil.

Acidic soils can be made more neutral by adding lime (at the rate recommended on the bag), while alkaline soils can be made more neutral by adding leafmold, peat moss, or compost on a regular basis. Extremely alkaline soil is the most difficult to rectify, and if you have this type of soil you might have to grow vegetables in raised beds or containers.

making compost

In the vegetable garden we tend to remove plants as they are ready to eat, so the soil is gradually impoverished. Making compost is a way of storing decaying plant matter until it has rotted down. It can then be returned to the soil, to add nutrients, amend soil texture, and help drainage.

compost bins

Compost bins can be made at home using wooden boards, plastic or wire netting, or bricks, or you can buy a range of bins, usually in plastic. Wood is the best material because it keeps the compost warm to help it rot and allows it to breathe. It is best to have three bins: one that you are filling up, another that is rotting down, and a third that is ready to use.

what to compost

- Use all garden waste and vegetable matter. Woody material will need to be shredded or chopped first.
- Use raw kitchen vegetable waste, including tea, coffee, and egg shells.
- Include newspaper, wood ash, torn cardboard, animal hair, and straw.
- Avoid perennial weed roots, such as quack grass or bishop's weed, and weed seeds.
- Avoid cooked food or nonvegetable food scraps, which will attract rats.

making compost

Pile all the material into the bin—the more you can put in at once, the more heat will build up to help rot the material. After a few weeks, fork the material out onto a plastic sheet, turn it to mix the contents, then pile it back in the bin. Repeat this from time to time until the compost is brown, crumbly, and sweet smelling. It is then ready to use.

where to grow vegetables

The traditional vegetable garden where the plants are arranged in long rows with bare soil in between is still used, but two other methods are perhaps better for beginning gardeners. The first is to grow vegetables in blocks instead of rows, and the second is to use raised beds.

block planting

Block planting is where the plants are arranged in blocks rather than long rows one plant deep. This allows closer planting and makes the ground more productive. Although the individual vegetables produced tend to be smaller, the overall yield is higher. The blocks should be a maximum of 4 ft. (1.2 m) across to allow you to reach all the plants without stepping on the soil. The disadvantage is that air circulation is better with rows, which helps prevent mildews and rust (see pages 42 and 44).

raised beds

Raised beds, with sides made from bricks or wooden boards, allow the soil to be deeply cultivated so that roots can go down a long way, not only providing extra stability but also increasing their chance of finding moisture in dry periods. Construct the beds no more than 4 ft. (1.2 m) wide so that you can reach all parts of the bed without walking on it. This maintains the structure of the soil and avoids the need for digging once the bed has been prepared.

Raised beds are good for gardens with poor soil because much of the mixture is brought in, allowing you to create a good, compost-rich, free-draining soil for your vegetables. If you have a raised bed across which you can easily reach, it makes sense to use block planting.

preparing beds

The only way to prepare a bed properly is to dig it, removing weeds, stones, and pests as you go. Fall is a good time in cold regions, because the frosts will break down the soil. Any remaining weed fragments that regrow can be removed before you start planting in spring.

where to site your vegetables

Don't just design your vegetable garden on paper. Have a good look at your yard and select a site that is open to the sun and the air, avoiding shady places under trees. Choose a warm spot away from frost hollows. You also need to check the soil to make certain that the drainage is good enough. If the soil does not drain freely, find another site because you will never successfully grow vegetables on waterlogged soil. Ideally, the soil should be rich, crumbly, and fertile, although this is less important as it can be amended and will be over the years of use.

clearing the ground

The next job is to remove any garbage left over from previous uses and any construction debris. It is also important to get rid of any weeds. If you have light soil, remove weeds by hand, but on heavier, clay soils this may be very difficult. You then have two choices: to cover the ground with black landscape fabric or an old carpet until the weeds give up (this will take some months, and in the case of perennial weeds at least a year); or to apply an herbicide. If used properly, you should need to use an herbicide only once.

digging the beds

Dig the soil thoroughly to a depth of at least 12 in. (30 cm), but preferably more. Remove any remaining weeds as you go and any trash you find buried. At the same time, dig in plenty of well-rotted organic material (see page 12). The deeper this goes the better because it will hold the moisture down near the roots, even when the top of the soil dries out. If the soil is very heavy, incorporate a lot of grit or fine gravel to improve the drainage.

last-minute preparation

The fall is the best time to prepare the bed. This gives any winter frosts the chance to break down the soil, making it easier to work with. It will also allow any remaining weed fragments to grow big enough to be seen, giving you the opportunity to remove them before you sow in spring.

In spring, rake over the dug soil, breaking it down to a fine tilth (a layer of fine, crumbly soil) and leveling the surface. Just before planting, rake in an all-purpose fertilizer, at the rate recommended on the package. Until you can recognize deficiencies in the soil from the appearance of the plants, it is best to check the soil with a good soil-testing kit and add fertilizers accordingly. You are then ready to start planting.

during the year

When you are replacing crops, such as lettuces, there is no need to do a full preparation before replanting. Remove all weeds and clear away any old leaves or remains of the previous crop. Lightly fork over the soil and rake it back to a fine texture. On light soils, particularly in dry conditions, it may just be sufficient to rake the surface over so that the soil is not disturbed, which will cause further moisture loss. At the same time, rake in a light dressing of fertilizer for the more hungry crops. In dry conditions, water well before replanting.

decorative vegetables

Most gardeners choose to keep their flowers and vegetables separate, but there is no reason why this should be so. Vegetables can be extremely decorative in their own right, so why not enjoy them in the garden as well as on your plate.

cottage-style garden charm

Cottage-style gardeners blurred the edges between decorative gardening and vegetable growing and often grew their vegetable plants and herbs in the flowerbeds. This was partly for practical reasons of limited space, and partly for the aesthetic benefits. Tepees of pole beans with their scarlet flowers, or globe artichokes with their bold, silver foliage, are just two great choices for the flowerbeds.

formal potagers

The idea of decorative vegetable gardens, or potagers, holds the most interest today. Here, the vegetables are not simply arranged in groups but also used in decorative patterns, with the textures, colors, and shapes of the plants exploited to make a satisfying picture. The shapes of the beds are often intricate, with formal paths between them and trained fruit trees adding permanent structure. Within the overall layout, the vegetables are planted in rows, blocks, or even singly, to create the desired pattern.

elegant edibles

If you want to make the most of the decorative qualities of vegetables, choose some of the following: scarlet-stemmed Swiss chard; bushy, sweet or hot peppers; bushy zucchini with green or yellow fruits; pole beans with prolific flowers in scarlet, white, or pink; and tomato plants with bright shiny fruits in red, orange, or yellow.

vegetables in containers

You don't need a big garden to grow vegetables. Even people with just a balcony can grow a few edibles because, with the right care, most are perfectly successful in containers.

choosing containers

Most containers are suitable. Large, plastic or ceramic pots, plain or decorative, are ideal and will look good on the patio, deck, or balcony. Less attractive, but cheap and practical, are old trashcans (ideal for potatoes), or even strong bags used by builder's suppliers to deliver materials such as sand. Another possibility is to build your own wooden containers. Whatever you do, keep in mind that the larger the container is, the less quickly it will dry out and the cooler the soil will be around the plant's roots.

getting the growing medium right

A soil-based potting soil is the best choice, because soilless mixes are too light and are difficult to rewet once they have dried out. Mix in plenty of humus in the form of well-rotted compost (see page 12), and improve the drainage by adding perlite, vermiculite, or grit. Put the container in place before filling as it will be heavy once it is full of moist potting soil.

where to stand them

Choose an open, sunny site in which to stand the containers. The permanent shade of a tree or tall building will not provide ideal conditions.

container care

Vegetables growing in containers will need regular watering to keep the potting soil just moist at all times. The watering will, however, leach (wash) the nutrients out of the soil, so apply a liquid fertilizer once a week when the plants are growing.

what and when to plant

If you have an enormous vegetable garden and a healthy
appetite, you can grow plenty of different varieties, but
most of us are restricted by space or time.

choosing vegetables

Concentrate on vegetables that are not easily available from supermarkets,
such as fresh snow peas or Jerusalem artichokes. Those that you use in
only small quantities, such as scallions, are also good choices. But perhaps
the best to choose are those that taste so much better when they are
fresh and home grown, such as sun-ripened tomatoes or waxy, yellow
early potatoes.

getting maximum yield

The key to vegetable gardening is to get the maximum out of your
garden. If space is limited, select varieties that don't take up much
space—globe artichokes, for example, need a lot of space for what they
produce. Intercropping also maximizes yield; this is when you plant fast-
growing crops, such as lettuces and radishes, between slower vegetables,
like Brussels sprouts or broccoli. The lettuces grow and are harvested
before the brassicas require the extra space.

Another way of maximizing yields is to sow another vegetable in the
space as soon as you have harvested the first.

don't overdo it

Resist the temptation to use all the seed in the packet. Only sow what
you can eat. It is better to sow a few lettuces, followed three weeks later
with another few, than to sow a large number all at once, which may
produce more than you require.

crop rotation

It is best not to grow the same crops each year in the same piece of soil, as the pests and diseases that attack specific crops will build up in the soil and become a problem. To avoid this, gardeners practice what is known as crop rotation.

how does it work?

Vegetables can be divided into four basic groups (see below), the members of which attract the same pests and diseases. Rotation involves dividing the space allotted to vegetables into four sections. You grow all the root vegetables or all the brassicas (the cabbage family) on one section one year, then move them to the next section the following year and so forth, returning to the original section in the fifth year. You don't actually have to have four individual sections—you can use the same large bed—but you move each crop to a different part of it each year. If you are growing vegetables in containers, change the potting soil every year.

what are the groups?

- **Legumes:** beans and peas.
- **Brassicas:** broccoli, broccoli raab, cauliflowers, Brussels sprouts, cabbages, kale, kohlrabi, rutabaga, and turnips.
- **Root vegetables:** potatoes, carrots, parsnips, celery root, Florence fennel, plus a few other related crops, including tomatoes, eggplants, peppers, and celery.
- **Onion family and the squashes:** garlic, leeks, onions, shallots, scallions, cucumbers, zucchini, summer and winter squashes.

Other vegetables can be slotted in with any of the groups where there is space, while permanent crops, such as rhubarb and asparagus, can have a space of their own.

propagation

Many gardeners start their vegetables off as young plants bought from a garden center or by mail order. This is by far the quickest way, but raising your own vegetables from seed is straightforward, satisfying, more economical, and you'll get a much bigger selection of varieties from which to choose.

getting started

The vast majority of vegetables are grown from seed. The exceptions are globe artichokes, rhubarb, potatoes, and Jerusalem artichokes (see page 34).

Buy seed fresh each year from a garden center or a supplier's online catalog. Reputable seed suppliers offer a much more exciting selection of varieties, and their catalogs are often useful sources of information. Seed can either be sown direct into the soil outdoors or in pots until the young plants are ready for planting outdoors.

sowing seed in the soil

Avoid sowing seed too early; wait until the soil has warmed up and dried out to prevent the seed rotting before it germinates. The ground is ready when the soil will break up into a fine, crumbly texture. Use a fork to turn over the soil, then rake it lightly to a fine texture, standing on boards if necessary to avoid compacting the soil.

Use a stake to mark out drills (narrow depressions) into which to sow the seed, consulting the seed packet to tell you how deep the drills should be. If the weather is dry, water the drills before sowing. Then sprinkle the seed thinly in the drills, cover by carefully drawing soil back to fill the drill, and firm down the soil gently with the back of your rake. Water well, using a fine spray to avoid dislodging the seed.

larger plants

Seeds of larger vegetables, such as parsnips, should be spot sown to avoid wasting seed. This means sowing two or three seeds where each of the mature plants will grow. Remove the excess seedlings at each spot, leaving just one strong plant. Another method is to sow the seeds as normal in a drill, then transplant the resulting seedlings into their permanent growing sites when their leaves are large enough to handle.

sowing in pots

Seed can be sown in pots or cell packs, indoors or in a greenhouse. This means that the seed can be sown earlier, and, by the time the soil is warm enough outdoors, the plants will be ready for planting out. Sowing in pots also stops mice eating the seed before it germinates.

Fill the pots with potting soil and shake them to settle the soil. Sow the seed thinly on top, before covering with a little more soil. Individual cell packs are a good idea as there is less root disturbance when you plant out. If you use cell packs, sow two or three seeds in each cell and thin to one seedling as soon as the seedlings emerge.

hardening off

Seedlings that have been grown under cover will need to be hardened off. This means getting them slowly acclimatized to the colder temperatures outdoors. Stand the seedlings outdoors for a few hours the first day, then bring them back indoors. Repeat, increasing the time spent outdoors for the next few days. After a week or so, the seedlings can be planted out.

other forms of propagation

Potatoes and Jerusalem artichokes are grown from tubers which should be laid in trenches rather than drills and spaced according to the variety.

Globe artichokes and rhubarb are increased by division. In early spring, lift a clump and break it into smaller sections, each with roots and at least one bud, which can be found around the edges of an old clump. Remove broken roots and replant clumps in new sites at the same depth as before.

fertilizing your plants

Nutrients are added to garden soil when it is being dug for vegetable growing. If you have prepared the ground thoroughly, there is rarely any real need to fertilize during growth, unless the plants are in containers.

why fertilize?

It is best, however, to fertilize your plants occasionally. Plants will not only grow bigger and be more prolific, but they will also be healthier and less susceptible to disease. This is important because preventing disease is better than curing it, especially if you want to avoid using chemicals.

all-important organic matter

The most important thing is to add organic material to the soil on a regular basis. This can be well-rotted garden compost or animal manure, both of which contain a good range of nutrients, as well as working wonders with the soil structure and encouraging all sorts of beneficial creatures, such as worms. Add organic matter when preparing the soil each spring, and you may not need any other fertilizer.

other fertilizers

Most gardeners, however, supplement organic matter with an all-purpose fertilizer. Liquid fertilizers are also useful, especially for container-grown plants, and for giving a quick boost as plants, such as tomatoes, are coming into fruit. There are organic liquid fertilizers available, too.

If you are worried about nutrient or mineral deficiencies in your soil, use a soil-testing kit to highlight any problems and then amend the soil by carefully choosing the right fertilizer.

watering

Water is essential for all plants, but especially for those producing vegetables. Indeed, all vegetables contain a large percentage of water. Deprive plants of water and at worst they die; at best, the vegetables are small and woody.

conserving water

Retaining water in the soil is the key, because the more you can conserve, the less you will have to add, saving time, money, and hard work. Adding organic material to the soil really helps hold moisture, so dig in as much as you can (see page 12). Organic material also works well as a mulch to prevent moisture evaporating from the soil surface— add a layer of well-rotted compost, leafmold, or even straw on the surface of bare soil. Inorganic mulches, such as black landscape fabric, also serve to prevent evaporation, but they are not especially attractive and they don't help to amend the soil.

how and when to water

Most water is provided by rain, but during prolonged periods of drought it may be necessary to water your crops, even when the soil is well mulched. Rainwater collected in rainbarrels is best, but municipal water is a good alternative. When watering, use a watering can or hose to soak the ground thoroughly. Sprinklers are very wasteful, but hand-held sprays or lances attached to a hose can be economical. Water when the surface of the soil is dry. Evening is the best time to water; avoid the heat of the day as the water will evaporate as soon as it hits the ground.

Containers dry out very quickly, especially small ones, so water when the surface of the potting soil is dry. In very hot weather, this will be once or even twice a day.

pests and diseases

Most gardeners get through life without much more than the occasional outbreak of blackfly or a mild case of mildew, and vegetable gardening is no different. Serious diseases in the vegetable garden are not common, especially if you practice good husbandry.

avoiding trouble

If you spot any diseased plants, it is usually easier to dig them up and discard them rather than trying to rescue them with doses of chemicals. Vegetables are short-term plants, so you can simply try again. On pages 42–4, there is a list of the most common pests and diseases. Remember that just because they are listed, it does not mean that your vegetables will suffer from them. With good husbandry and common sense they won't succumb. The key to success is to keep plants healthy so they aren't susceptible to problems like pests and diseases.

   If you are not growing from seed, buy young plants from a reputable supplier and never plant what may look like diseased plants, especially brassicas. Always make certain that the plants have optimum growing conditions: plenty of light, plenty of air (but not strong winds), plenty of water, and nutrients. Don't allow the growth of your plants to be checked in dry weather: mulch the ground and water regularly to keep the plants moist and growing strongly.

   Another important factor is to keep a well-balanced garden. Many pests have their own natural predators: for example, ladybugs, lacewings, and hoverflies demolish vast numbers of aphids, while ground beetles eat slugs and underground larvae. If you have flowerbeds with a wide range of plants, you are likely to attract many different creatures to the garden. These will create a balance, and you should rarely have problems.

Aphids There are hundreds of different types of these sap-sucking pests, but they rarely cause serious problems. If you have a large infestation, rub the stems through your fingers to squash them or blast them away with a jet of water.

Birds These attack young seedlings. Try bird scarers or netting, although a wire cage is the only way to keep them away with any certainty.

Blight A problems with only tomatoes and potatoes, this infectious disease causes brown marks on the tops of leaves and stems and white spores underneath. Prevent it by buying resistant varieties and good-quality seed potatoes. Space plants widely for good air circulation. Discard affected plants; do not add them to the compost pile.

Cabbage rootfly This serious pest affects mainly brassicas. The adults lay eggs near the plants, and the pupae burrow into the soil to eat the roots, causing wilting and poor growth. Prevent the pupae from burrowing by planting young plants through a layer of floating row cover or fine mesh on the soil, or surround each plant with a tightly fitting root collar after planting.

Caterpillars Caterpillars affect many crops, but mainly brassicas. Cover the crops with floating row cover to prevent butterflies laying eggs or simply pick off the caterpillars as they appear.

Clubroot A serious disease of brassicas and some root vegetables, clubroot causes distortion and swellings on the roots. If your brassicas are inexplicably wilting, dig one up and check the roots. If you find clubroot, dig up and discard the entire crop. Prevent the disease by rotating crops (see page 30), and making your soil slightly alkaline (above pH7). Buy young plants from a reputable supplier or grow your own from seed.

Downy mildew A fungal disease causing discolored patches on leaf surfaces and fluffy, white or gray growth beneath. It thrives in warm, damp conditions. Remove and destroy affected leaves, improve air circulation, and water at the base to avoid spreading it.

Top left: Aphids. Top right: Blight.
Bottom left: Caterpillars. Bottom right: Clubroot

Flea beetles These small, shiny, jumping beetles leave tiny holes in leaves and stems, and the larvae eat the roots, weakening plants. Prevent an attack by growing crops under insect-proof mesh.

Mice, groundhogs, and gophers Mice will eat peas and beans from the soil after sowing, while groundhogs and gophers cause havoc, burrowing beneath the vegetables. Live trapping is the best control method.

Powdery mildew A whitish, powdery fungal growth appears on leaves and stems. Keep plants well watered, and make sure there's plenty of air circulation to prevent it. If it appears, remove and discard affected leaves.

Red spider mite Rarely a problem in the open garden, but more commonly seen in greenhouses. The tiny, red or brown mites suck the sap and cause leaves to become silver, then yellow. They thrive in dry conditions, so keep the atmosphere moist and humid by spraying the plants and by regularly watering the greenhouse floor.

Rust This fungal disease attacks only a few plants, including leeks and beans, causing yellow or brown pustules on the foliage. Ignore it as it does not cause any problems.

Slugs and snails Probably the most severe problem for many gardeners. The best method to clear them is to go out at night with a flashlight and destroy any you find. If you don't mind using chemicals, slug pellets are also effective.

Viruses There are many different types, all incurable. They usually appear as stunting and distortion of the plants, with unusual color changes or patterning on the leaves, such as mottling or mosaic patterns. Viruses are spread by aphids or by the gardener and his tools. Keep aphids at bay and buy resistant varieties. If viruses occur, remove affected plants.

Whitefly Rarely a problem in the open garden, more of a problem in the greenhouse, these tiny, sap-sucking insects can be controlled by hanging up yellow sticky fly traps or by using a biological control.

Top left: Flea beetles. Top right: Powdery mildew.
Bottom left: Rust. Bottom right: Whitefly

protecting crops

There are several ways to protect crops from cold weather and marauding pests. A barrier of glass or clear plastic forces a much earlier crop than from plants in the open garden, and insect-proof mesh will keep flying pests at bay.

Cold frames Cold frames are like small, low greenhouses. They can be covered with an old blanket at night to maintain a good temperature. They are also useful for hardening off young plants (see page 34).

Floating row cover This light, woven fabric is used to protect plants from frosts, especially in late spring. It is also a good choice for preventing insects getting at young seedlings.

Greenhouses Vegetable plants can be grown in a greenhouse in the same way as they are in the garden. In cold regions, it is also a good place to start off tomatoes, eggplants, and other tender crops, which benefit from the protection and raised temperatures early in the growing season. A heated greenhouse can be used to germinate and raise seeds before it is warm enough to sow them outdoors.

Hoop houses and cloches These are transparent covers used to protect single plants or whole rows in the garden, keeping the soil and air around the plants a little warmer. Glass cloches are more expensive than plastic cloches or low hoop houses. Plants under protection need circulating air to prevent fungal diseases. Be sure to water regularly as the soil will dry out more quickly than in an open environment.

Micromesh This is a fine netting used to protect crops from insect pests, such as caterpillars and carrot rust fly. It allows light to reach the crops so it can be used as permanent protection.

harvesting and storing produce

The moment you pick your first home-grown vegetable is always exciting, but the first taste is even more of a thrill.

when to harvest

As a general rule, the less time between harvesting and eating the better as the flavor and vitamin content start to deteriorate as soon as vegetables are picked.

It is usually obvious when vegetables are ready to harvest, and many are even sweeter if you pick them while they are small, so there's no harm if you are a little early. If you are unsure whether they are ready, pick a handful and try them.

Many vegetables have a definite end to their harvesting season, and they become tough or woody as they age, so be sure to harvest them before this point and store the produce while it is in peak condition.

Some vegetables, including leeks, cabbages, and cauliflowers, can be left in the ground until you are ready to use them. Most root crops will tolerate at least some cold weather, so dig them up when you need them. Parsnips actually taste a little better after a frost, so leave them until you have had a cold spell.

storing produce

After harvesting, store vegetables in a cool but frost-free place, preferably with air circulating round them. Open boxes or mesh sacks are ideal. Some root vegetables, including carrots and potatoes, should be surrounded by sand or peat moss.

Most vegetables can be frozen after harvesting. Canning and pickling are also great ways to preserve vegetables, which can be enjoyed later in the year. Specific details of when and how to harvest can be found under the entry for each vegetable.

getting growing

garlic

Garlic is a vital ingredient in many cuisines around the world and presents few problems to the grower. One of the advantages of growing your own is that you can harvest some of the heads while still green and juicy, to appreciate their fresh flavor in your spring cooking.

Site & soil Garlic does best in a sunny, open site and a light soil. If your soil is heavy, dig in plenty of organic matter and grit or fine gravel. to improve the drainage. Garlic needs a moderately rich soil, so plant in ground to which compost or manure was added for the previous crop earlier in the spring or the fall before. Avoid recently fertilized ground.

Sowing & planting Garlic is grown by planting individual cloves split from a bulb. It is best to buy a specific cultivar from a specialty seed supplier that suits your conditions. For best results, plant cloves in late fall as they need two months at a temperature of 32–50°F (1–10°C). Garlic can also be planted in late winter. It generally takes 26–35 weeks from planting to harvest.

Plant individual cloves with the flat basal plate at the bottom of a small hole, with the pointed tip about 1 in. (2.5 cm) or so below the soil surface. Space at 6 in. (15 cm) intervals, with about 12 in. (30 cm) between rows, or 8 in. (20 cm) each way if you are planting in blocks (see page 18).

Care Keep the area free from weeds. It is best to weed by hand to avoid damaging the bulbs with a hoe.

Problems Garlic is generally trouble free, although it may suffer from various fungal diseases. The most common are rust (see page 44) and onion white rot, which causes the leaves to turn yellow and wilt. If you lift a bulb you will see fluffy, white fungus with little, black specks on the roots. It can stay in the soil for a considerable time, so be sure to rotate crops (see page 30). If disease does occur, dig up infected plants and discard them. If it is close to harvest time, however, ignore any rust, but remove all infected parts of the plant when you lift the bulbs.

Harvesting Harvest fall-planted garlic in early or midsummer as the leaves turn yellow; dig up late-winter-planted garlic a bit later. Dry the bulbs and remove any soil before storing. If you want fresh, green garlic, lift the immature bulbs while the leaves are still green.

Storing Store in a cool, dry place with good air circulation, for example in string sacks or bags. The bulbs can be tied in decorative strings, but don't hang them in a warm kitchen, as they will not last long. Some varieties store longer than others, so check the suppliers' catalogs when you buy.

Good choices California Late, Elephant, Inchelium Red, Polish White, Silver Rose, Spanish Roja

leeks

Leeks are among the mainstays of the winter kitchen, perfect for warming soups and casseroles. They can be left in the ground until required, and with the right selection of cultivars you could be enjoying fresh leeks from the fall through spring.

Site & soil The ideal site is open, with well-drained, water-retentive soil, which does not become waterlogged in winter. Try raised beds (see page 18) with plenty of humus.

Sowing & planting Leeks can be sown in pots under cover and then planted out, or sown directly in the soil and then transplanted. They generally take 16–20 weeks from sowing to harvest.

Sow thinly in flats or cell packs in a good-quality seed starter mix and place in a cool greenhouse. Harden off (see page 34) and plant out when the leeks are 8 in. (20 cm) tall. Space the leeks 4–6 in. (10–15 cm) apart in rows 12 in. (30 cm) apart. Alternatively, grow in blocks with leeks set 6–9 in. (15–23 cm) apart. Make holes 5–6 in. (12–15 cm) deep and lower each leek into one. Do not refill the holes with soil, but fill them with water.

If sowing direct, sow seed in drills (see page 32) from early spring and transplant to their permanent positions in the same way as pot-grown plants.

Care Once the leeks have filled their planting holes, they can be hilled to blanch the stems by gently drawing soil

up around the leeks to exclude light. Keep the area weeded by hand to avoid damaging the leeks with a hoe.

Problems Rust (see page 44) is the most common problem for leeks, and it can be identified by a golden powder on the leaves. It is not serious and can be ignored. Keep the leeks watered in dry weather and avoid close planting to prevent rust. Plants may bolt, that is produce flower stems, and this results in a hard center to each leek. Again, watering in dry weather will prevent this.

Harvesting Leeks can be left in the ground until they are required. Some early cultivars may go soft as the winter progresses, so sow later crops as well, to give a long period of good-quality leeks.

Storing Leeks are best left in the ground; they do not keep well once lifted.

Good choices Alaska, American Flag, Blue Solaise, Durabel, King Richard, Lincoln, Musselburgh, Pandora, Neptune, Swiss Giant–Zermatt, Titan

onions

Onions are probably the most useful vegetable in the kitchen, and if you grow your own you will always have plenty to hand and a choice of different sizes. Onions can be grown from seed or from small bulbs called sets.

Site & soil Onions prefer an open, sunny site. The soil should be well drained and reasonably fertile. Incorporate compost or manure into the soil in the fall for spring planting, and in spring for fall planting.

Sowing & planting Onions can be grown from seed, or planted as small bulbs called sets. Sow seed in flats or cell packs under glass in winter, then plant the seedlings in the garden in spring. Alternatively, sow direct into the soil in shallow drills (see page 32) in spring, or in late summer for an early crop.

Plant sets in late winter if the soil is not waterlogged, or in early spring. Space them 4 in. (10 cm) apart in rows 12 in. (30 cm) apart, or 6 in. (15 cm) apart if you are planting in blocks (see page 18). The tips should be just visible above the soil. You can also buy sets for fall planting, and these produce earlier crops. Onions generally take 18–42 weeks from sowing/planting to harvest, depending on method.

Care Weed the area carefully by hand to prevent bulb damage. Be careful not to loosen the bulbs in the soil while weeding.

Problems Onions can suffer from onion white rot (see page 54), downy mildew (see page 42), and onion neck rot, which doesn't usually appear until after the bulbs have been harvested. They become soft and a gray, fluffy mold develops around the neck.

All these can be prevented by crop rotation (see page 30) and good hygiene. Problems can also be reduced by ensuring a good flow of air round the plants by wide spacing. Removal of infected plants will help prevent spread. Seedlings seem to be less susceptible than sets.

Onion fly may also be a problem, as the maggots bore holes into the bulbs and eat the roots. Avoid onion fly by covering with insect-proof mesh soon after the sets have been planted.

Harvesting Allow the leaves to fall over and die back, then carefully loosen the bulbs from the soil. Leave them lying in the sun for a few days for the skins to ripen.

Storing Keep in a cool, dry place, preferably hanging in nets or string bags, or tie into ropes so that the air can circulate between bulbs. Do not hang ropes in a warm kitchen, unless you use them quickly, as they will soon shrivel. Open wooden boxes with slatted sides are another good choice.

Good choices Alisa Craig, Candy, Copra, Early Yellow Globe, Kelsae, Long Red Florence, Red Baron, Red Pearl, Snowball, Snow White, Superstar, Vidalia, Walla Walla, White Prince, Yellow Granax

shallots

Shallots grow in little clusters of bulbs, smaller and milder than regular onions. They are invaluable in slow-cooked casseroles and are deliciously sweet when roasted. They are also used in oriental dishes and raw in salads. Stored well, they will last throughout the winter.

Site & soil Shallots prefer an open, sunny site, but will tolerate a little shade. The soil should be free draining and reasonably fertile. Ground that had compost or manure for a previous crop is ideal. Alternatively, add compost or manure in the fall before planting.

Sowing & planting Shallots are usually grown from small bulbs called sets. Plant the sets in late winter or early spring. In warm, dry areas it can be earlier, even late fall or early winter. Shallots generally take 20–28 weeks from sowing/planting to harvest.

Push each set into a hole in the soil, so that a little of the bulb tips are just above the soil surface. Plant at 6 in. (15 cm) intervals with rows set about 10 in. (25 cm) apart. Space sets about 8 in. (20 cm) apart if you are growing in blocks (see page 18).

Shallot seed is now also available, but it will produce single bulbs rather than clusters. Sow in shallow drills (see page 32) and thin seedlings to 2 in. (5 cm) apart.

Care Keep the area well weeded, preferably by hand to avoid damaging the bulbs with a hoe. Take care not

to dislodge the bulbs at the same time as the weeds. Water in dry weather when the bulbs are swelling.

Problems Shallots can suffer from the same problems as onions (see page 62), but on the whole they are less troublesome. At the early stages, the newly planted bulbs may pop out of the ground, either pushed out by the emerging roots or by birds looking for nesting material. Make certain that bulbs are planted up right to their tips, and replant any that come lose.

Harvesting Let the foliage die back naturally, then lift the clusters of bulbs. As with onions, lay shallots in the sun for a few days for the skins to ripen. Once they rustle when rubbed, split the clusters into individual bulbs.

Storing Keep over winter in a cool, dry place, storing the shallots in net or string bags, or in slatted, open boxes. The air must be able to circulate round them. They can also be plaited into ropes, but avoid hanging in a warm kitchen, where they won't keep well.

Good choices Ambition F1, Bonilla, Golden Gourmet, Holland Red, Mikor, Olympus, Pikant, Prisma F1, Red Sun

scallions

Scallions, also known as bunching onions, make a crisp and flavorsome addition to salads. They can also be used in sauces and cooked dishes, particularly in Oriental cuisine. Pickling onions are grown in the same way, except they form small bulbs.

Site & soil Scallions like an open, sunny site, although they can be grown in the lee of a tall hedge as long as it does not overhang them. They like an open, free-draining soil that is not too fertile; soil that had compost or manure for a previous crop is ideal. Scallions grow best in regions with cool, spring weather and hot, dry summers. Pickling onions can be grown in poorer soil. Raise early crops under cover in a hoop house, cold frame, or greenhouse if you have one. Scallions are also good vegetables for growing in containers.

Sowing & planting Sow outdoors from early spring until early summer, or under cover from midwinter to late summer. Scallions and pickling onions generally take eight weeks from sowing to harvest.

They should be sown thinly in shallow drills (see page 32) about ½ in. (1 cm) deep, with the rows about 6 in. (15 cm) apart. If the soil is dry, water along the base of the drill before sowing.

Thin the seedlings to about ¾ in. (2 cm) apart when they appear. If you are growing in blocks (see page 18), thin to ¾ in. (2 cm) apart in both directions.

Care Little attention is required, other than weeding. Take care not to disturb the scallions as they can easily be pulled up with the weeds. Water during dry weather.

Problems Scallions and pickling onions can suffer from the same pests and diseases as onions (see page 62), but as crops mature quickly these are rarely a problem. If disease does strike, remove the whole plant and start again in new soil. The onions can become tough if they become too dry, so water in dry weather.

Harvesting Scallions can be harvested as soon as they are large enough to use. They can usually be pulled from the ground by hand, but in heavier soils they may require a hand fork to lift them. Pull alternate onions and allow the neighbors to continue growing. Pickling onions should be left until the foliage dies down, then lifted.

Storing Leave in the ground until required; scallions do not store well for more than a couple of days. Pickling onions can be dried and stored for a short time before pickling.

Good choices Evergreen Hardy White, Guardsman, Ishikura Improved, Ishikuro, Paris Silverskin, Purplette, Red Baron, Tokyo Long White, White Lisbon

broccoli raab

Broccoli raab is a wonderful mainstay for winter cooking, although the season can last from the fall until spring. The tender, young spears, or florets, stand the frost well and make a delicious treat or side dish drizzled with butter or anchovy dressing.

Site & soil Choose an open, sunny site protected from the wind, as this can loosen the large, heavy plants. They will grow in any reasonably fertile soil; soil that had compost or manure the previous fall is ideal. If your soil is acid, add some lime to bring the pH up to 6.5–7 (see page 14).

Sowing & planting Sow seed in spring under cover in flats or cell packs, or in the garden. Broccoli raab generally takes 8–12 weeks from sowing to harvest.

   In the open ground, sow in drills ½ in. (1 cm) deep, then thin the seedlings to about 2 in. (5 cm) apart in the row.

   When the seedlings are 5 in. (12 cm) tall, transplant them into their permanent positions. Those grown under cover should be hardened off first (see page 34). Water the plants the evening before transplanting. Plant deeply in rows or blocks with 24 in. (60 cm) between plants. Make certain the plants are firmly planted by pressing down the soil with your heel. Keep watered until established.

Care As with all vegetables, keep the ground free of weeds. As this is a long-term crop, mulch to prevent weeds and to conserve water (see page 38). Water during dry periods, especially as the spears form.

Problems Cabbage rootfly (see page 42) can be troublesome; cover the seedbeds and young transplants with floating row cover or transparent, insect-proof mesh to avoid the problem. Caterpillars (see page 42) can be a real nuisance; cover the plants with mesh or pick off the caterpillars as they appear. Clubroot (see page 42) is a problem with all brassicas. It is difficult to cure, so prevention is important—buy plants only from a reliable supplier or grow your own to avoid infection.

Harvesting Pick the young spears as they appear. The flowers should be in tight bud—once they start to show yellow they are opening and no longer suitable for picking.

Storing Pick the broccoli spears as you require them, as they are difficult to store fresh for more than a few days. If you have to keep them, stand the spears in water and keep in a cool place. Broccoli raab freezes well.

Good choices Bordeaux F1, Early Purple Sprouting, Early White Sprouting, Late Purple Sprouting

calabrese

Known by most people as "broccoli," calabrese is similar to broccoli raab but the flowerheads are much larger and arranged in a smooth, rounded head. Romanesco has heads made up of pointed whorls of flower buds. Both are highly nutritious and flavorsome vegetables.

Site & soil As with most brassicas, these vegetables need a sunny, open site protected from the wind to avoid root movement. Calabrese will tolerate a less fertile soil than broccoli raab; soil that has had compost or manure added the previous year is ideal. Add lime to the soil (see page 14) to bring the pH up to around 6.5–7 to help reduce the chances of clubroot (see page 42).

Sowing & planting Calabrese resents root disturbance, so it cannot be sown in rows and then transplanted. Sow in cell packs or fiber pots, or spot sow in open ground (see page 34). Sow seed in spring. Calabrese generally takes 14–20 weeks from sowing to harvest.

Space plants 6 in. (15 cm) apart in rows 12 in. (30 cm) apart, or if you are growing in blocks (see page 18) space plants 9 in. (23 cm) apart.

Care Keep the area weeded, but avoid disturbing the plants. It is important to water during prolonged dry spells, especially as the heads begin to develop.

Problems Calabrese suffers from the same diseases and pests as other brassicas. Keep watered in dry weather and do not plant too close together, to avoid downy mildew (see page 42). Caterpillars (see page 42) can be prevented by covering plants with a fine mesh or by picking off by hand. As calabrese is a short-lived plant, either ignore other diseases, or dig up and discard plants.

Harvesting Cut off the central head, including some stem, as the buds form but before they open into flowers. Sideshoots will develop into smaller heads, and these can be harvested as required.

Storing Remove heads as required. They can be kept for a few days by placing the cut stem in water and keeping them in a cool place. Calabrese freezes well.

Good choices Beaumont F1, Belstar F1, Coronado Crown, Early Dividend, Fiesta F1, Green Comet, Green Goliath, Kabuki, Natalino, Packman, Romanesco, Veronica

cauliflower

With its beautiful, white curds, cauliflower looks like no other vegetable. Home-grown cauliflower is crisper and sweeter than its supermarket equivalent, and there are many different varieties from which to choose, including yellow, purple, and green forms.

Site & soil Choose an open, sunny site away from strong winds. As some varieties overwinter outdoors, avoid frost pockets. Soil should be of medium fertility—perhaps having had compost or manure added for a previous crop. If your soil is acid, add lime to bring the pH up to 6.5–8 (see page 14).

Sowing & planting Varieties of cauliflower for harvesting at different times of the year all need sowing at different times. Their planting distances also differ, so when buying seed check the recommended times and distances. Cauliflower generally takes 16–40 weeks from sowing to harvest.

Seed can be sown in flats or cell packs under cover, or in the garden in drills ½ in. (1 cm) deep. Thin seedlings to 2 in. (5 cm) intervals when they appear.

Transplant young plants to their permanent positions, spacing at the distance recommended on the seed packet, or to 24 in. (60 cm) apart. Use your heel to push the soil down to firm well around the plants. Water well.

Care Keep the area weeded. Water well during dry spells or the heads may be encouraged to flower quickly and

become lose. Mulching will help retain moisture in the soil (see page 38). As the heads begin to mature, break the leaves so they cover the head to keep the curds white.

Problems Cauliflower suffers from the same pests and diseases as other brassicas, clubroot (see page 42) being the most serious. Rotate crops (see page 30) and either buy plants from reliable suppliers or grow your own to avoid clubroot. Caterpillars (see page 42) can be picked off by hand, or cover plants with fine, insect-proof mesh to prevent butterflies laying their eggs. Cabbage rootfly (see page 42) can be prevented with tightly fitting root collars or by keeping the plants covered with floating row cover or fine mesh.

Harvesting Cut the head when the curds are tight and white. Once they begin to open, they are past their best. Once the head has been cut, remove the whole plant as it will not produce further heads.

Storing Use soon after cutting, or store for a few days in a refrigerator and use before the heads start to become discolored. Heads can also be hung upside down in a cool place for two weeks or so. Alternatively, break the heads into florets and freeze.

Good choices Amazing, Apex, Candid Charm F1, Cheddar, Early White, Fremont F1, Gipsy, Graffiti F1, Snow Crown, Veronica, Violet Queen, White Excel F1, Winter Aalsmeer, White Cloud

brussels sprouts

When freshly picked, lightly boiled, and drizzled with butter, Brussels sprouts are a revelation. There are many different varieties providing a range of flavors, including sweet ones which particularly appeal to children.

Site & soil As with most vegetables, Brussels sprouts prefer an open, sunny site. Choose an airy place, to prevent mildew, but one that is protected from wind, which could otherwise blow the plants over. Brussels sprouts can be grown in any reasonable soil with an average fertility, such as soil that has had compost or manure added from a previous crop. Add lime to raise the pH to 6.5–7, to help prevent clubroot.

Sowing & planting Sow in flats or cell packs under cover, or in a seedbed in the garden. For early crops, sow under cover in early spring, followed by the maincrop in spring to early summer. Outdoors, sow in drills ½ in. (1 cm) deep, and thin plants to 2 in. (5 cm) once the seeds have germinated. Brussels sprouts generally take 9–12 months from sowing to harvest.

Plants are ready for transplanting 5–6 weeks after sowing. Harden off (see page 34) those raised under cover before planting in the garden, at 24 in. (60 cm) intervals, in rows 30 in. (75 cm) apart. If growing in blocks (see page 18), space young plants 24 in. (60 cm) apart. Plant in firm ground and use your heel to push the earth down firmly around each plant.

Care Generally, Brussels sprouts need little care apart from weeding around them. Remove any yellow or dying leaves, and pull off some of the green leaves as the sprouts mature, to improve air circulation.

Problems Besides the problems seen in other members of the cabbage family (see page 90), Brussels sprouts can suffer from bolting, where the heads become very loose and open. Planting in firm, not loose, soil helps. Also plant the young plants deeply, up to the first leaves, to deter cabbage rootfly (see page 42) and cover with floating row cover. Pick off any caterpillars by hand. White mealybugs can cause problems: the fluffy, white bugs stick on the stems and sprouts. Treat with insecticidal soap. Aphids can also be a problem (see page 42).

Harvesting Pick when the sprouts are big enough, removing the leaves to make it easier. Snap the sprouts downward to free them, starting at the base of the stem. Most varieties taste better after a frost. The cluster of leaves at the top of the stem is also very tasty.

Storing Brussels sprouts are best used as soon as they are picked. They can be kept for a few days, but lose their freshness. The whole stem can be picked and hung in a cool place, or stood in water, for up to a week. They freeze well for longer storage.

Good choices Diablo, Falstaff, Jade Cross, Long Island Improved, Nelson F1, Oliver, Prince Marvel, Red Bull, Red Rubine, Tardis, Tasty Nuggets, Topline, Trafalgar, United, Valiant

cabbage

Whether it's a dark green, curly Savoy or a colorful, red one, cabbage is as delicious as it is healthy giving. There are many different varieties, varying with the type of head, the time of harvest, and the color, so grow a selection.

Site & soil Choose an open, sunny site protected from strong winds. Cabbages can be grown in most soils, but preferably those that have not recently had compost or manure added. Ground enriched for a previous crop is ideal. The pH should be around 6.5–7 (see page 14), so add lime if your soil is acidic.

Sowing & planting The different types of cabbage are sown at different times of the year, so follow the recommendations on the packet. For example, spring cabbage is sown in late summer. Cabbages generally take 20–40 weeks from sowing to harvest.

Sow in flats or cell packs under cover, or thinly in drills ½ in. (1 cm) deep, in the garden. Thin seedlings to 2 in. (5 cm) apart, when they emerge. When the plants are large enough to handle, transplant into rows or blocks, following the planting distances recommended on the packet. Firm the soil around each plant with your heel.

Care Ensure the area is kept free of weeds. Refirm the ground if the cabbages are rocked by the wind. Water regularly in prolonged dry spells and apply a mulch of

well-rotted compost or leafmold if necessary, to retain moisture (see page 38).

Problems Cabbages are more troublesome than most other vegetables, but you probably won't encounter any serious pests and diseases. Caterpillars (see page 42) can be a nuisance—remove them by hand or cover plants with insect-proof mesh to prevent egg laying.

Take preventive action against clubroot (see page 42) by liming the soil to raise the pH (see page 14), and by either growing your own plants or obtaining them from a reliable supplier. Protect overwintering plants against birds using netting. Cabbage rootfly (see page 42) can be prevented by placing a tightly fitting root collar around the base of each plant.

Harvesting Cut the cabbages as they are required. Lift the whole plant or cut the stem just below the head. Spring cabbages should be cut from the stem, as these may produce a second crop.

Storing Winter cabbages are bred to withstand cold weather, so leave them *in situ* until required. Once cut, they can be kept in a cool place for several days. Some of the dense winter varieties will last several weeks, even months, hung in nets in cool, airy conditions protected from frost.

Good choices Clarissa, Danish Bullhead, Derby Day, Dynamo, Earliana, Greyhound, Hispie, Hispie Pixie, Holland Winter White Extra, Jade Pagoda, January King, Mammoth Red, Minicole, Minuet, Multikeeper, Red Jewel, Red Rookie, Ruby Perfection, Savoy King, Stonehead, Super Red 80, Tundra

kale

Available in a range of vivid colors and strange shapes, kale makes an attractive addition to the flower garden. It can be substituted for cabbage or spinach. Kale is a very hardy plant that withstands cold winter temperatures, and is extremely rich in vitamins.

Site & soil Choose an open, sunny site with good air circulation. Avoid a windy place for the larger varieties of kale, as windrock can be a problem. Most garden soils are suitable, as long as they are not too rich—perhaps use soil that has had compost or manure added for a previous crop. If necessary, add lime (see page 14) to bring the pH up to 6.5–7.5

Sowing & planting Sow crops for summer harvesting in flats or cell packs under cover in late winter; transplant in spring when they are large enough. Kale generally takes 7–40 weeks from sowing to harvest.

Sow fall and winter crops in spring in the garden in drills ½ in. (1 cm) deep, then thin the emerging seedlings to about 2 in. (5 cm) apart. Kale can also be sown in flats or cell packs under cover. Transplant the young plants into their permanent site, spacing them 24–30 in. (60–75 cm) apart, or at about half this distance for dwarf kale or if you intend to harvest the leaves when young.

Care As with all vegetables, ensure that weeds are kept at bay. Mulching (see page 38) helps to suppress weeds as

well as retain moisture in the soil during dry periods. Water thoroughly during prolonged dry spells.

Problems During late summer and the fall, caterpillars can be a threat: pick them off by hand or cover plants with insect-proof mesh. Birds can be a problem in winter, so protect the plants with netting. Cabbage rootfly (see page 42) can be avoided by using a root collar around the base of each plant.

Kale can also suffer from cabbage whitefly: the tiny, white adults fly away when disturbed, while the brown young stay on the undersides of the leaves. They result in sticky honeydew and sooty molds on the foliage but are rarely serious. Wash light infestations from the plant with a spray of water; for more serious outbreaks, spray with insecticidal soap.

Harvesting Pick the leaves as they are required, either while they are young and fresh, or more mature and flavorsome. They sometimes have more taste after a frost.

Storing Kale is very hardy and will withstand most winters, so don't harvest until required. The leaves do not store well, but they can be frozen successfully.

Good choices Black Tuscany, Darkibor, Dwarf Blue Curled, Dwarf Green Curled, Redbor, Red Russian, Toscana

fava beans

With their fresh, distinctive flavor, fava beans are delicious in a wide range of dishes, including risotto and warm salads. The fresher they are the better they taste, so growing your own gives you a distinct advantage. They can also be successfully grown in containers.

Site & soil Fava bean plants require an open, sunny site. Fall-sown crops will have to stand through the winter so may need protection from strong winds to prevent windrock problems. Fava beans will grow well in most garden soils as long as they are not too wet or too dry. The soil should be reasonably fertile and will benefit from having well-rotted compost or manure added.

Sowing & planting Sow in late fall for early crops the following year, if your climate is not too wet or cold. Otherwise, sow from late winter to late spring, depending on the variety. Fava beans generally take 12–30 weeks from sowing to harvest.

Make a trench about 1½ in. (4 cm) deep and 6 in. (15 cm) wide, and sow two staggered rows, spacing the beans about 6 in. (15 cm) apart. Rows should be 24 in. (60 cm) apart. If you are planting in blocks (see page 18), space the beans 10 in. (25 cm) apart. You can also sow them in individual pots and plant the young plants out at the same distances.

Care Protect fall-sown beans against the wind and cover with hoop houses in wetter areas. Weed carefully, being

certain not to disturb the beans' roots. Taller varieties may need strings along either side of the row to hold the plants upright.

Problems Watch out for mice stealing the sown beans. Cover the rows with wire cages, or grow the beans in pots and plant out as young plants; or trap the mice. Aphids (see page 42) may also occur on the young tips of the plants around flowering time. The best remedy is to pinch these tips out, either before the problem arrives or after they are infested. The other possible nuisance is rust (see page 44). This looks bad but rarely causes a problem. However, remove plants immediately after harvesting and clear away any remains, to help prevent recurrence.

Harvesting You can begin harvesting as soon as the fava beans are big enough. Smaller beans have a better flavor, and the larger they get the more floury they become. You can also eat the young pods of some varieties.

Storing Fava beans are best eaten straight from the plant while at their maximum sweetness. They do not keep well once picked, as they lose their flavor. They freeze well (do this straight after picking). Alternatively, allow the beans to dry in the pods on the plants, then store them in an airtight jar.

Good choices Aquadulce, Broad Windsor, Cascine, Con Amore, Green Windsor, Imperial Green Longpod, Jubilee Hysor, Sweet Lorraine, The Sutton

bush beans

Probably the most versatile beans for cooking, bush beans
come in a range of colors, from green and yellow to purple.
These are plants that grow to only 12 in. (30 cm) or so tall,
and include kidney beans, lima beans, and snap beans. They
are nutritious and perfect for stir-fries and salads.

Site & soil Choose an open, warm, sunny site protected
from strong winds. Bush beans can be grown in most
garden soils, but a rich, light soil suits them best. Enriching
the soil with compost or manure in spring helps produce a
good crop. Bush beans can also be grown very successfully
in containers.

Sowing & planting Wait until the soil and air temperatures
have warmed up. Temperatures below 50°F (10°C) will
inhibit germination and cause the seedlings to die. If
in cold regions you want an early crop, sow in pots under
cover and transplant once temperatures rise, or grow in
containers under glass. Bush beans generally take 7–14
weeks from sowing to harvest.

To sow in the garden, make a trench about 1½ in. (4 cm)
deep and 6 in. (15 cm) wide, and sow two staggered rows
within the trench, spacing the beans about 6 in. (15 cm)
apart. Rows should be 24 in. (60 cm) apart. If you are
planting in blocks (see page 18), space the beans 8 in.
(20 cm) apart. You can also sow bush beans in individual
pots and then, after your last expected frost date, plant the
young plants in the garden at the same distances.

Care Weed carefully around the plants, as they can be easily uprooted. Protect in windy areas to prevent root disturbance. The taller varieties are best supported by twiggy sticks or lines of strings held on stakes.

Problems There is a long list of diseases from which bush beans can suffer, but unless you are unlucky most rarely seem to cause trouble. One of the most likely problems is the seed being stolen by mice. Cover the seedbed with wire cages, or sow in pots and then plant the young plants in the garden, to overcome the problem. Slugs and snails may eat the emerging shoots, but once the plants are mature they are less vulnerable.

Harvesting Pick bush beans as they become large enough, with the little stalk still on the bean. The more you pick, the more they will produce. Old beans become tough, but they can be dried.

Storing Bush beans are best cooked and eaten straight from the plant. They will keep for a few days, but soon start to lose their quality. For long-term storage, blanch and freeze them. Some varieties will produce beans inside the pods if allowed to mature: dry them and store in an airtight jar until required.

Good choices Blue Lake, Borlotto, Carson, Ferrari, Golden Teepee, Hestia, Kentucky Wonder, Maxibel, Pencil Pod Wax, Provider, Purple Queen, Purple Teepee, Royal Burgundy, Speedy, Tenderette, Tendergreen, Tricolor, Vermont Cranberry, Yin Yang

pole beans

Any vigorous vining bean that grows by twining itself around a support is known as a pole bean. Runner beans, some of which have the advantage of being "stringless," are more suitable than lima beans for cool regions. Both are simple to grow.

Site & soil Choose an open, sunny site away from strong winds, as the plants cover a large area once trained up a support. The soil should be fertile, but any good garden soil will do, especially if you dig in well-rotted compost or manure the previous fall. Avoid more recently enriched ground, as this may encourage foliage at the expense of flowers and beans. Pole beans grow well in containers.

Sowing & planting Pole beans need warmth to germinate and grow, so don't sow them before the soil and weather warm up. If you are impatient, sow in pots under cover a couple of weeks before it is warm enough outdoors, and plant in the garden when the young plants are big enough and there is little risk of frost. Pole beans generally take 14–26 weeks from sowing to harvest.

Sow the beans in pairs about 2 in. (5 cm) deep. If both germinate, remove the weaker seedling. Plants should be spaced 6 in. (15 cm) apart, either in a single or double row or around a tepee of poles.

Care Pole beans need support. Erect a double row of bean stakes, a tepee of poles, or use a framework of supporting

strings. They need to be at least 6 ft. (2 m) tall. The plants are self-supporting, but may need to be trained at the start. Keep watered in dry weather.

Problems On the whole, runner beans are fairly trouble free. See page 102 for problems affecting lima beans. Poor flower set may be a problem, due to the weather keeping pollinating insects away or birds pecking the flowers. Water shortage can also cause flower drop, so keep plants well watered in dry weather.

Harvesting Pick the beans as soon as they are big enough to eat. The more you pick the more they will produce. Pole beans can become "stringy" and tough if they get too old, so pick regularly, even if it means giving the beans away, as there are too many for your own use. Discard any beans that have got too big.

Storing Cook as soon as possible after picking, for the best flavor. Beans will keep a couple of days in a cool place, but not more than that. If you want to store them for winter use, blanch and freeze them, or try salting beans by slicing the pods and packing layers into airtight jars with layers of salt in between.

Good choices Achievement Merit, Blue Lake, Borlotto Firetongue, Fortex, Garden of Eden, Goldfield, Kentucky Blue, Kentucky Wonder, Kwintus, Lady Di, Marvel of Venice, Northeaster, Purple King, Romano, Scarlet Emperor, Trionfo Violetto, Wisley Magic

peas

Peas are among the most popular of vegetables, yet surprisingly few people grow them. Eaten raw straight from the pod, fresh, home-grown peas are far sweeter than any you can buy. Peas are easy to grow, as are snow peas and snap peas, which are treated in the same way.

Site & soil An open, sunny site is ideal, although peas will also tolerate a little shade. Since the plants are often tall, avoid windy places. The soil should be well drained but moisture retentive, preferably with a reasonable amount of humus in it (see page 12). Shorter varieties of pea can be grown in containers.

Sowing & planting For an early crop, sow in early spring, ensuring that the soil is not waterlogged. Otherwise, sow from mid- to late spring, once the soil has started warming. Peas generally take 12–16 weeks from sowing to harvest.

If you want to start early, or if you have problems with mice, sow in pots or cell packs under cover and plant out as young plants with as little root disturbance as possible.

In the garden, sow peas in a single or double, staggered row at 2 in. (5 cm) intervals. Double rows should be 9 in. (23 cm) apart with at least 24 in. (60 cm) between rows. Only short varieties of pea are suitable for planting in blocks (see page 18).

Care Peas need support—choose branched, twiggy sticks, plastic netting, or wire netting. Short varieties can be grown

up the same supports, or just stretch horizontal strings on either side of the row. Water in dry weather.

Problems Mice and birds can eat the peas before they germinate: cover the rows with wire cages, which will also protect the young plants from rabbits. Mildew (see pages 42–4) can be a problem if air circulation is poor, but ignore it unless it is very severe. Pea moths may be troublesome; they are revealed as maggots in the pods. Sow early and late to avoid them, and cover the row with insect-proof mesh when plants are in flower.

Harvesting Pick the peas once they have swelled in the pod, and keep picking to encourage a continuous supply. Peas become floury and hard if they are left too long on the plant. Pick snow peas as the pods develop and reach an edible size; harvest snap peas when the pods swell.

Storing Cook or eat immediately after picking if possible. The quality deteriorates the longer they are stored, so use within a couple of days at most. Peas often produce sudden gluts that provide too many to eat, so freeze the excess. Peas can be left on the plant until the pods become dry and the peas rattle in them—pick them, dry them, and store in a jar until required for soups and casseroles.

Good choices Alderman, Ambassador, Blondie, Green Arrow, Little Marvel, Maestro, Mr. Big, Pioneer, Strike, Zipper Cream
Snow peas: Carouby de Maussane, Dwarf Gray Sugar, Mammoth Melting Snow, Oregon Giant, Oregon Sugar Pod,
Snap peas: Amish Snap, Cascadia, Sugar Ann, Sugar Lace, Sugar Snap, Sugar Sprint,

asparagus

Asparagus is an easy and trouble-free plant to grow at home, and is so much sweeter and more delicious straight from the garden than from the supermarket. Drizzle with melted butter, or serve with fried eggs and shavings of Parmesan cheese. It is also wonderful in risotto, pasta dishes, and salads.

Site & soil Choose an open, sunny site away from strong winds, as the fully grown plants can suffer from windrock. The soil should be free draining and not too rich; most garden soils are suitable.

Once planted, asparagus can remain in the soil for many years, so prepare the soil well before planting, improving drainage if necessary and removing all traces of perennial weeds.

Sowing & planting Asparagus can be grown from seed or from crowns, which are the fleshy roots. Crowns produce spears earlier, and they are often more reliable plants. Asparagus generally takes three years from sowing to harvest, and one year from planting crowns to harvest.

Sow seed under cover in late winter in cell packs, then plant the young plants in the garden in early summer. Alternatively, sow in drills in the garden in spring, thinning seedlings to 6 in. (15 cm) apart.

Plant crowns or young plants in the garden in spring. Make a trench 10 in. (25 cm) deep with a ridge down the middle. Rest the crowns on the ridge, with their roots spread out on either side. Cover the crowns with 4 in.

(10 cm) of soil and add more as the plants grow, until they reach soil level.

Care Make certain that the area is kept free from weeds, but be careful not to damage the plants' roots. Remove all old foliage as it turns yellow.

Problems Generally, asparagus does not suffer from any problems, although asparagus beetle can be a nuisance by eating foliage and stunting growth. The beetles overwinter in plant debris so clear up well around the plants. Hand-pick the larvae or spray them with a jet of water. Slugs can also be a nuisance and should be cleared, using your preferred method. Violet root rot can also be a problem. Dig up and discard any affected plants.

Harvesting Allow the plants to develop for the first couple of years, picking only a few spears. From the third year after planting, harvest more heavily. Cut all spears during the harvest period (about eight weeks) so that there is a constant renewal. Harvest the spears when they are 6 in. (15 cm) above the surface, cutting them off up to 2 in. (5 cm) below soil level.

Storing Asparagus is wonderful when eaten really fresh, so delay picking until just before cooking. It will keep in the refrigerator for a couple of days with the bases of the spears in water, but the flavor deteriorates after picking. Any excess can be frozen.

Good choices Connover's Colossal, Jersey Knight, Jersey Supreme, Martha Washington, Purple Passion, UC 157, Viking KB3

globe artichokes

Cutting your own artichokes is one of the great luxuries of vegetable gardening. As well as producing something delicious to eat, these are also very attractive plants and add stature to the vegetable or flower garden. They are a pleasure to grow, and produce very few problems.

Site & soil Choose a sunny, open site, although globe artichokes will tolerate a little shade. Protect from high winds. They will grow in most garden soils, but avoid wet soils and those waterlogged in winter. Globe artichokes appreciate a relatively rich soil, so dig in well-rotted compost or manure before planting. Since the plants will be in the ground for a number of years, be sure to remove all traces of perennial weeds before planting.

Sowing & planting Globe artichokes can be grown from seed but the resulting plants are very variable. It is much better to buy young plants. They generally take 16–36 weeks from planting to harvest. Plant in midspring, leaving 3 ft. (1 m) between plants. Trim the leaves back to 6 in. (15 cm).

Plants will be productive for three or four years, so after the third year dig up one plant and split it up into divisions, replanting the best ones into new soil. Remove the other old plants once the new ones are established. Repeat every three or four years.

Care The most important thing is to keep the area well weeded, being especially vigilant for perennial weeds. Mulch

(see page 38) to prevent the plants drying out in warm weather, and in colder regions add a winter mulch to protect plants against frost.

Problems Globe artichokes are not subject to pests and diseases. The weather can be the only real problem—high winds may damage the plants, but this can be prevented by choosing a sheltered site or by adding some form of protection. Waterlogged soils also cause problems, which again can be avoided by choosing the right site or by improving drainage before planting.

Harvesting Cut the flowerheads when they are large enough to eat, removing around 4 in. (10 cm) of stem with them. Harvest only when the scales are still tight to the heads—it is too late when the scales become loose or the flowers begin to open.

Storing Pick the artichoke heads as required. They will keep for a couple of days in a cool place but are much better when fresh. If you have a glut, cut off the scales and freeze the hearts.

Good choices Green Globe, Imperial Star, Violetta di Chioggia

kohlrabi

With a crisp texture and a delicate flavor somewhere between a cabbage and a turnip, kohlrabi can be grated raw into salads, or be steamed and used as a summer alternative to turnips. There are varieties with green and purple skins, some of them growing very large.

Site & soil Choose a sunny, open site in the garden, or grow under cover, in a greenhouse or under a hoop house, for an early crop. Kohlrabi does best in light soils, especially those that are not too rich—a plot enriched for a previous crop is ideal. They also do well in containers or grow bags.

Sowing & planting For an early crop, sow in cell packs under cover in late winter. When they are 2 in. (5 cm) tall, plant kohlrabi in a greenhouse, under a hoop house, or in the open garden when the weather is not too cold or wet. Kohlrabi generally takes 5–8 weeks from sowing to harvest.

Alternatively sow in the garden in drills ½ in. (1 cm) deep, in rows 12 in. (30 cm) apart. Thin the seedlings to 6–7 in. (15–18 cm) apart, as they emerge. If planting in blocks (see page 18), space plants 10 in. (25 cm) apart.

Sow further crops under cover in early fall for winter use. Choose purple-skinned varieties, as these are hardier.

Care Kohlrabi should be kept in continuous growth, so water regularly in dry weather if necessary. Keep the area weeded, but be careful not to disturb the roots.

Problems Although it is the swollen stem that is eaten, kohlrabi is in fact a member of the cabbage family, although it is not so susceptible to the diseases from which brassicas tend to suffer. It is a relatively quick crop to mature, so fairly trouble free, although it may become tough if allowed to dry out too much. Control slugs (see page 44) while the plants are small, and check for flea beetles (see page 44) at the same time.

Harvesting Pull up the kohlrabi as you need it. It is best while small; once it gets older and larger, it may become woody and tough. Some of the purple-skinned varieties can grow very big without this toughness.

Storing If possible, use the vegetable as soon as you harvest it. Kohlrabi will store for some days after pulling, but its freshness soon deteriorates. Late crops can be stored for a couple of months in slightly damp sand in a frost-free place, or be left in the soil until required if they are growing under cover.

Good choices Azur Star, Early White Vienna, Kolibri F1, Kossack Lanro, Purple Danube, Purple Vienna, Quickstar F1

rutabaga

Rutabaga is a true winter treat when added to soups and casseroles, or when made into a golden mash oozing with butter and black pepper. It survives well in the ground over winter, so is always on hand when you require some fresh vegetables.

Site & soil Like most vegetables, rutabaga does best in an open, sunny site. It prefers a light, well-drained soil, but will grow well on most garden soils as long as it is not waterlogged. The soil should not be too rich—soil to which compost or manure has been added for a previous crop would be ideal. Avoid freshly turned soil, as rutabaga prefers to be sown in a firm soil. Lightly press the soil down if you have just dug it.

Sowing & planting Don't be tempted to sow too early in the growing season: late spring is early enough in most regions. Rutabaga generally takes 24 weeks from sowing to harvest.

Sow in drills ¾ in. (2 cm) deep, in rows 15 in. (38 cm) apart. Sow in ground that has been firmed down, not in loose soil. While the seedlings are still small, thin them out to about 9 in. (23 cm) apart. If sowing in blocks (see page 18), space the plants 12 in. (30 cm) apart. If you intend to harvest crops when the roots are still quite small, rutabaga can be grown closer together.

Care Keep the area well weeded, as rutabaga is often in the ground for nearly a year and weeds can build up during this time. Water regularly and consistently during dry weather, otherwise the roots become tough and woody, and a sudden resumption of watering may lead to cracking.

Problems Rutabaga belongs to the cabbage family and can suffer from all the same pests and diseases (see page 90), but it is generally free from trouble. Flea beetle (see page 44) can be a problem with young seedlings, so sow seed under insect-proof mesh. Slugs can also be troublesome while plants are young. If you have clubroot (see page 42) in the garden, rutabaga is likely to catch it. Try to prevent infection by raising all your own brassicas from seed rather than buying plants. Mildew (see pages 42–4) can also be a nuisance, so ensure the plants have air circulating between them and keep them watered.

Harvesting Rutabaga can be lifted as required, as soon as the swollen roots are big enough. As these grow above ground, they can easily be pulled.

Storing Rutabaga is winter hardy in mild regions and can be left where it is until required. However, in late winter roots tend to become woody, especially in mild weather, so it is often best to lift them. Store in net bags or boxes in a basement or garage, or leave in piles in the garden covered with a generous layer of straw.

Good choices American Purple Top, Burpee's Purple Top, Helenor, Marian, Magres, Thompson Laurentian, Virtue

turnips

Like kohlrabi and rutabaga, turnips belong to the cabbage family. They are mainly grown for their crisp, white roots, perfect for casseroles and stir-fries, but the young leaves (the turnip tops) can be used as a delicious spring green, at a time when fresh vegetables are in short supply.

Site & soil Unlike most vegetables, turnips will tolerate a little shade. The soil should be moisture retentive because they can become woody and tough if they dry out too much. Choose soil that has had compost added for a previous crop, because turnips prefer soil that is not too rich.

Sowing & planting Turnips should be sown *in situ* as they do not transplant well. For summer crops, sow from early spring. In colder areas, use row covers; alternatively, sow unprotected from midspring onward. Turnips generally take 6–12 weeks from sowing to harvest.

Sow summer varieties until late spring, fall varieties after that. Sow a batch every three weeks for a continuous crop if you use a lot of turnips. Sow in drills ¾ in. (2 cm) deep, in rows about 12 in. (30 cm) apart. Thin the seedlings to 6 in. (15 cm) apart, as they emerge; leave them slightly closer for quick-maturing varieties. For block planting (see page 18), space plants 6 in. (15 cm) apart.

Care Ensure turnips are watered regularly during a dry spell or they will become hard and woody. They are also likely to bolt. Keep the area weeded, as weeds will take up moisture.

Problems Turnips are prone to many of the same pests and diseases as other brassicas. Generally, however, they suffer few troubles, especially if they are pulled young before any problems develop. Flea beetles (see page 44) may be a problem for young seedlings: cover the seedbed with insect-proof mesh or floating row cover. Slugs may also be a nuisance at this stage.

Harvesting Harvest as soon as the roots are big enough to eat. Turnips are best pulled while still relatively small, as the bigger they get the tougher and more woody they become. Harvest the leaves as greens when the plants are young, or remove all growth from turnips still in the ground in late winter to promote new leaves, which are excellent for eating.

Storing Leave turnips in the ground until they are required. In colder areas, however, they can be lifted and stored in a cool basement or garage in net bags or boxes. Alternatively, make them into a neat pile outside and cover with straw.

Good choices Hakurei, Oasis F1, Purple Top Milan, Snowball, Tokyo Cross, White Lady

parsnips

These sweet, starchy root vegetables are a great winter standby and will happily stay in the ground until you fancy a buttery mash, a warming soup, or some crisp, roasted chunks. Or if you can't wait, pull them as minivegetables and steam them whole to enjoy their fresh flavor.

Site & soil Choose a sunny, open site. The soil should be light and not too rich—one fertilized the previous year is ideal. Make sure the soil is deeply dug and as stone free as possible, otherwise the parsnips will be forked and stunted, rather than the classic cone shape, making them more difficult to deal with in the kitchen.

Sowing & planting Buy seed fresh each year for a good germination rate. Parsnips are slow to germinate, so sow some radishes thinly in the same drill, to mark the row and make weeding easier. Parsnips can be sown from late winter to late spring, but early spring is the best time. They generally take 24 weeks from sowing to harvest.

Sow in drills ¾ in. (2 cm) deep, in rows 12 in. (30 cm) apart. Spot sow (see page 34) three seeds at 5–6 in. (12–15 cm) intervals. Thin seedlings to one per spot, as they emerge. For block planting, thin seedlings to 6–8 in. (15–20 cm) in each direction.

Care As parsnips are in the ground for a long period, keep the area free from weeds. Be careful in the early stages, as the seedlings are easily disturbed.

Problems Canker is probably the most serious problem for parsnips, causing brown woody patches on the roots. To prevent it, avoid sowing seed too early, make certain the soil is not too rich, and add lime if conditions are too acidic—aim for a pH of 6.5–7.5. If parsnips do get canker, cut off the cankerous bit and eat the rest. Carrot rust fly (see page 142) may also attack, but rarely damages large parsnips very much. Covering the seed with insect-proof mesh after sowing will reduce the problem.

Harvesting Dig up the parsnips as they are required. For the best flavor, wait until after the first frost. If you want miniparsnips, however, pull when they are the desired size.

Storing Leave parsnips in the ground until they are required. In areas with severe frosts, cover the rows with straw to keep the soil from freezing so that you can dig them up when needed. When they start shooting in spring, however, they should be discarded. Therefore, dig up the remainder before then, cut into battens, blanch, and freeze.

Good choices All American, Andover, Gladiator F1, Harris Model, Javelin F1, Lancer, Tender & True

beet

Whether long or round, red, yellow, or white, beet is a joy in the kitchen, for salads, soups, purées, risotto, and casseroles. It is also simple to grow and suffers very few problems. This is a great plant for containers.

Site & soil Beet prefers an open, sunny site. It will grow in most garden soil, but does best in light, rich conditions. Soil that has had compost or manure added for a previous crop is ideal. Beet can be grown under cover in containers for early crops, or in containers on the patio or deck.

Sowing & planting Most packets of beet seed contain small clusters of seeds, producing groups of seedlings that need thinning early on, to prevent too much root disturbance of the remaining plant. Beet generally takes eight weeks from sowing to harvest.

Beet can be sown early under cover in cell packs and planted out, but it is easier to sow *in situ*. Sow in drills ½ in. (1 cm) deep, in rows about 12 in. (30 cm) apart. Spot sow (see page 34) the seed in twos at 4 in. (10 cm) intervals. Thin seedlings as soon as possible, leaving one at each spot. For block planting (see page 18), thin beet seedlings to 6 in. (15 cm) apart. Continue to sow at three-week intervals to produce a continuous crop of small beet throughout the growing season.

Care Keep the area weeded but be careful not to disturb the roots at an early stage of their growth. If a prolonged

dry spell sets in, keep the plants watered so they continue to grow steadily.

Problems Beet is generally trouble free and easy to grow. Slugs may be a problem when the plants are still young, and they can also damage beet overwintering in the ground.

Harvesting Beet are easy to harvest—simply pull them from the ground as soon as they have reached the desired size and are needed. Smaller ones are more succulent, but larger ones are still edible, although they tend to get tough as winter progresses.

Do not cut off roots or leaves, as this will cause the beet to bleed when cooked. Remove the leaves by twisting them off about 2 in. (5 cm) above the swollen part of the root. Remove the rest of the root after cooking.

Storing Usually it is possible to leave beet in the ground until required, but they may become tough. Slugs may also attack them. Cover with straw in colder areas to prevent the ground freezing, making them difficult to pull. Beet freezes well once blanched, and young beet can be pickled for winter use.

Good choices Albina Vereduna, Bull's Blood, Burpees Golden, Chiogga, Crimson Globe, Cylindra, Detroit Dark Red, Kestrel, Lutz Green Leaf, Moneta, Nero Tondo, Pablo F1, Pronto, Red Ace F1, Ruby Queen, Sparkler

carrots

Freshly pulled and crunchy, there is nothing to match the flavor of home-grown carrots. Carrots come in a wide range of colors, including yellow, white, and purple, as well as the more common orange. They are also available in round or long, tapering varieties.

Site & soil Choose an open, sunny site. Carrots have a preference for light, well-drained soils, but will grow in other soils. Dig the soil deeply and remove as many small stones as possible, as they cause the carrots to fork—round carrots are better in stony soil. If you have a heavy, clay soil, make a conical hole for each plant, fill with a light compost, and sow the seed in the top.

Sowing & planting Carrots will not germinate below a temperature of 46°F (7°C), so wait for the soil and air to warm up before sowing. Initial sowings, in early spring, can be protected from severe frost under a hoop house or floating row cover. Carrots generally take 12–15 weeks from sowing to harvest.

Sow very thinly in drills ½ in. (1 cm) deep, in rows at least 6 in. (15 cm) apart. Thin the seedlings to about 8 cm (3 in) apart, preferably in the late evening when carrot rust flies are not around (see page 142). If growing in a block, thin seedlings to 4 in. (10 cm) apart.

Sow at two- to three-week intervals to get a succession of crops throughout the summer and into the winter.

Care Keep the area weeded but be careful not to disturb the roots when they are young. Do not bruise the foliage, or you risk attracting carrot rust flies (see below). Water regularly in dry weather to keep the roots succulent.

Problems The chief problem is carrot rust fly, the larvae of which bore into the roots. Choose a variety that has some resistance to this pest, and sow thinly, so that you don't have to thin the seedlings, as the smell of bruised foliage attracts the flies. It is also wise to thin carrots in the late evening when the flies are less active, and to bury the thinnings deep in the compost bin, to hide their smell. Slugs can also be troublesome, especially in winter.

Harvesting Carrots can be pulled as soon as they have reached the desired size. Pull the first of the season when they are quite small, though, as they have a very distinctive and wonderful flavor.

Storing Carrots can be left in the ground until you want them. However, they are difficult to dig up during severe frosts, so cover the rows with straw to prevent the ground freezing, or dig them up and store them in a cool garage or basement in boxes of sand. They also freeze well.

Good choices Autumn King, Bolero, Canada Gold, Chanteney Red-cored 2, Crème de Lite, Danvers Half Long, Early Nantes 5, Flyaway F1, Hercules, Honeysnack, Imperator, Minicor, Mokum F1, Nantes Half Long, Paris Market, Parmex, Primo F1, Purple Haze F1, Rainbow F1, Siroco F1, Thumbelina, Touchon, White Satin, Yellowstone

salsify and black salsify

These unusual root vegetables are not often seen in supermarkets, yet they are delicious and easy to grow. Both have a subtle flavor; that of salsify is faintly reminiscent of oysters, while black salsify has a delicate, nutty flavor. They are grown in the same way, much in the manner of parsnips.

Site & soil These two vegetables need an open, sunny site. In its second year, salsify will produce beautiful, purple flowers and looks good when grown in flowerbeds. Both have long, straight roots and need a deep soil, preferably free draining. Avoid stony ground or the roots will become forked. If you have heavy soil, make a conical hole for every plant, fill it with a light compost, and sow the seed in the top, to give a free root run.

Sowing & planting Do not sow too early as the seed will rot if the ground is too cold. Salsify and black salsify generally take 20 weeks from sowing to harvest.

In midspring, in a trench ½ in. (1 cm) deep, spot sow salsify seed (see page 34) at 8 in. (20 cm) intervals; space rows about 12 in. (30 cm) apart. Sow two or three seeds at each spot and thin to one seedling as soon as possible. If you are planting in blocks (see page 18), spot sow at 9 in. (23 cm) intervals. Black salsify can be sown slightly closer together.

Care Keep the area well weeded, but avoid disturbing the plants when they are still at seedling stage. Weed by hand

rather than using a hoe, which may damage the maturing roots. Water during prolonged dry periods.

Problems Both vegetables are trouble free and easy to grow.

Harvesting Dig the roots when they are big enough to eat, which will not be before the fall. Dig carefully as they are relatively thin and can easily break. Black salsify may not get big enough in its first year and can be left in the ground until the second.

   The leaves of both vegetables can be blanched in spring by covering the plants with a deep mulch. Pick the emerging leaves and use them like chicory.

Storing Both salsify and black salsify are usually left in the ground until required. After digging, they will keep for a few days in a cool place or will store for up to two months in a box of just-damp sand.

Good choices Both salsify and scorzonera are usually sold by seed merchants as just that. There are rarely individual varieties available, although salsify is sometimes labelled 'Sandwich Island' and scorzonera may be offered as 'Duplex'.

potatoes

If you have only ever eaten supermarket potatoes, you won't realize the range of different potato flavors available. As well as the different varieties, each with its own unique flavor, there is the unbeatable taste of the first potatoes of the season, freshly dug and lightly boiled.

Site & soil Potatoes are easy to grow and not too demanding with regards to conditions: an open site is best, but they will tolerate a little shade. They will grow in most soils, but do best in a light one. The soil should be relatively rich, but not recently amended.

Sowing & planting Potatoes are planted as tubers, or "seed potatoes"—buy fresh, disease-free stock each year. Before planting, allow the seed tubers to presprout by placing them in egg cartons with most of the "eyes" uppermost. Keep in a bright place, out of direct sunlight, at 64°F (18°C), then move them to a cooler place when they start to sprout. When the shoots are 1 in. (2.5 cm) long, after six weeks, they are ready to plant. Potatoes generally takes 15–20 weeks from planting to harvest.
Dig a trench 6 in. (15 cm) deep and set the potatoes in it 12 in. (30 cm) apart, with 18 in. (45 cm) between rows. Cover the potatoes, then draw the soil up over each row to form a mound.

Care Hill the rows by covering any shoots that show with more soil. Keep the soil free of weeds, and water during

periods of drought. If frosts are still likely after the leaves of early potatoes have come up, cover them with floating row cover, straw, or newspaper.

Problems The most serious is blight (see page 42), a fungal disease that also affects tomatoes. Hill the rows to help prevent spores getting to the tubers. If blight attacks, remove all infected foliage at once and discard it, then leave the tubers in the ground for at least three weeks.

Slugs may eat holes in the tubers, especially those left too long in the soil. Remove the slugs and lift the tubers as soon as possible, to reduce the problem. Minimize the chance of diseases by always buying certified varieties and by rotating the crop to fresh soil each year (see page 30).

Harvesting Dig the first early potatoes as soon as they are about 1 in. (2.5 cm) across, when the plants come into flower. Maincrops are harvested once the foliage begins to die down. Leave the potatoes on the surface of the soil for at least a few hours, to dry the skins.

Storing Lift all the potatoes at the onset of the fall and store them in a cool, frost-free place. Store in burlap or paper sacks. It is important that the tubers are protected from light, or they will go green and become toxic. Only store disease-free tubers.

Good choices Adirondack Blue, All Blue, All Red, Bison, Butte, Butterfinger, Caribe, Charlotte, Desiree, Kennebec, Maris Piper, Red Norland, Red Pontiac, Rose Finn Apple, Russian Banana, Silverton Russet, Yukon Gold

jerusalem artichokes

With their distinctive, nutty flavor and starchy texture, Jerusalem artichokes are perfect for soups, casseroles, and purées, or simply sliced and sautéed in butter. Most people are surprised to learn that the Jerusalem artichoke is, in fact, a sunflower.

Site & soil Grow Jerusalem artichokes in an open, sunny site if possible, although they will tolerate a little shade. Avoid a windy place, as they can grow quite tall. Most garden soils are suitable, but avoid badly drained or poor soils—light soils make harvesting easier.

Sowing & planting Jerusalem artichokes are grown from tubers. They generally take 16 weeks from planting to harvest.

Dig a 6 in. (15 cm) deep trench and place a tuber every 12 in. (30 cm) along it. Remember to plant tubers with the buds facing upward. Draw the soil back over the trench and gently firm it down. Set the rows at least 3 ft. (1 m) apart, as the plants become quite tall. If you are planting in blocks (see page 18), set the tubers in individual holes, about 18 in. (45 cm) apart.

Care Jerusalem artichokes are very easy to grow. Weeding is the main activity, but be careful not to hoe off the emerging shoots, especially while they are still just below the surface. Hand weeding is safer. Draw soil some distance up the stems as they grow to help support the

plants. In windy areas, support the stalks with strings or wires fixed to a stake at each end of the row. Toward the end of summer, cut off the top half of the stems to reduce windrock.

Problems Jerusalem artichokes are generally trouble free. Slugs, however, may be a problem, especially as the artichokes are usually left in the ground until required. The only other problem is likely to be subsequent crops, as even the smallest piece of tuber left in the ground will grow again. Be sure to clear them thoroughly at the end of the season if they are not to become a nuisance.

Harvesting Dig the tubers as required any time after the leaves have begun to wither. Try to remove every tuber from each plant at a time, even if they are too small for the kitchen; otherwise, as explained above, they will regrow.

Storing Generally there is no question of storage as Jerusalem artichokes can be left in the ground until required. In really cold areas, where winter digging is difficult, dig all or some of the tubers and store in a cool place in a box of just-damp sand.

Good choices They are normally simply sold as 'Jerusalem artichokes', although there is one named variety, 'Fuseau', which produces regular-shaped tubers.

celery root

With its nutty, celerylike flavor, celery root can be grated raw into salads or served cooked, perhaps sliced and baked with cream and hot peppers, or boiled and mashed with butter. This delicious vegetable is relatively easy to grow and stores well, so it is always on hand when needed.

Site & soil Celery root prefers an open, sunny site, but will tolerate shade. Since it remains in the soil all winter, avoid planting in frost pockets. The soil should be fertile and moisture retentive without being waterlogged. Humus-rich soil is ideal—dig plenty of compost into the soil in the fall.

Sowing & planting In cold regions, it is best to sow celery root under cover. If you wait until the frosts have finished before sowing outdoors, the bulbs will not have time to develop before winter sets in. Celery root generally takes 26 weeks from sowing to harvest.

Sow in cell packs in a heated propagating unit in late winter or early spring, or in a cool greenhouse in midspring. When the seedlings are big enough to handle, transfer to individual pots and grow on. Once the threat of frost has passed, harden off the plants (see page 34) and plant them in the garden at 12 in. (30 cm) intervals in rows about 15 in. (38 cm) apart. Use the same distances if planting in blocks (see page 18).

Care Weed carefully around the plants, preferably by hand. Keep watered if the weather turns dry, as celery root

dislikes dry conditions. As the celery root begins to mature, remove the lower leaves so that the bulb is exposed.

Problems In the early stages after planting in the garden, watch out for slug damage. Celery root rarely suffers from any other pests and diseases, but it may catch the same diseases that affect celery (see page 162). If you are worried about celery leaf miner (see page 162), keep the plants covered with insect-proof mesh or floating row cover.

Harvesting Lift the bulbs once they have swollen to a decent size, any time from late summer onward. The longer they are in the ground, the more flavor they have so don't start harvesting too soon.

Storing Celery root can be left in the ground until it is required. In colder areas where winter digging is difficult, cover the rows with straw or, if necessary, lift the bulbs and store in a cool place in a box of just-damp sand.

Good choices Brilliant, Diamant

celery

Celery is invaluable in the kitchen, served raw in salads and with cheese, or cooked in soups, casseroles, and sauces. It can even be braised as a vegetable in its own right. The "trench" varieties have the best flavor, but newer, self-blanching and green varieties are quicker and easier to grow.

Site & soil Choose an open, sunny site if possible, although celery will tolerate a little shade. It prefers a light, moisture-retentive soil—soil enriched the previous fall is ideal. Avoid waterlogged conditions.

Sowing & planting Sow the seed under cover in cell packs in early to midspring, then transfer to individual pots when the seedlings are big enough to handle. Harden off (see page 34) and plant out the young plants after the threat of frosts is over. Celery generally takes 15–20 weeks from sowing to harvest.

Plant self-blanching and green varieties in blocks, with plants spaced 10 in. (25 cm) apart, so that the plants blanch each other, that is exclude light to make the stems white.

As the name suggests, trench varieties used to be planted in a shallow trench, then the soil was drawn up around the stems to blanch them as they grew. Nowadays it is more usual to plant trench celery on flat soil, but use cardboard sleeves covered with black plastic and tied with string to exclude light from the stems. Plant celery 14 in. (35 cm) apart with 30 in. (75 cm) between rows.

Care Watering must be consistent if celery is not to become stringy, so be sure to water regularly in dry periods and never let the soil dry out.

As already described, tie light-excluding sleeves made from cardboard and plastic around trench varieties, to keep the stems white as they grow. Tuck some straw around self-blanching varieties when they are about 8 in. (20 cm) tall, to help exclude light.

Problems Slugs are the biggest threat, both at planting and harvest time. Celery leaf miners can also be troublesome, but these are rare. They tunnel into the leaves and stems, causing a tracery of brown. Remove and destroy affected foliage. Celery will become stringy and tough if deprived of nutrients or moisture, so keep well watered and apply high-nitrogen fertilizers regularly.

Harvesting Harvest before frosts strike, simply digging up the clumps. Trench varieties can stay in the soil a bit longer.

Storing Celery is usually pulled as it is needed, although it will keep for a few days in a refrigerator. If you have to harvest a lot at once, store in a cool place, preferably in a box of just-damp sand. You can also move plants to a greenhouse and roughly replant them until required.

Good choices Afina, Florida, Galaxy, Golden Self-blanching, Par-cel, Picador, Tango F1, Tendercrisp, Utah 52-70, Ventura, Victoria F1

florence fennel

Fennel is useful not only for its aniseed-flavored bulb, which can be sliced raw in salads or cooked in pasta dishes, risotto, casseroles, and bakes, but also for its feathery foliage, which makes an excellent herb to accompany fish and chicken dishes.

Site & soil Fennel needs a warm and sunny site sheltered from the wind. The soil should be moisture retentive, as fennel does not like to dry out, but avoid waterlogged conditions. A humus-rich soil is ideal, but it shouldn't be too rich—a site amended for a previous crop would be perfect.

Sowing & planting Sow under cover in midspring in cell packs. As soon as the threat of frost is over, plant fennel in the garden, causing as little root disturbance as possible. Space plants at 12 in. (30 cm) intervals, in rows 12 in. (30 cm) apart.

Alternatively, sow directly into the garden in late spring or early summer, sowing a batch every three weeks to get a succession of crops. Fennel generally takes 12 weeks from sowing to harvest. Make drills ½ in. (1 cm) deep, and spot sow several seeds at 12 in. (30 cm) intervals (see page 34). Leave at least 12 in. (30 cm) between rows. If planting in blocks (see page 18), space plants 12 in. (30 cm) apart.

Care Keep fennel well watered—it resents drying out and will quickly bolt (come into flower) if it does. As the bulbs begin to develop, hill them by drawing soil up round the

bulbs to roughly half their height, to prevent them getting too tough.

Problems Slugs can be a threat, especially to seedlings and young plants. The other major problem is lack of water, which will cause plants to bolt and produce flowers at the expense of the growing bulb. Make certain there is plenty of humus in the soil to retain moisture, and water regularly if there is no rain.

Harvesting When the fennel bulbs are about the size of a tennis ball, cut them off just above the base. The roots usually resprout to produce new foliage, which can be used in a variety of dishes and salads.

Storing Florence fennel is usually harvested as it is required as it will not keep long after cutting. It will tolerate a little frost, but by the onset of winter it is usually past its best. Once fennel is cut, it can be kept for a few days in the refrigerator.

Good choices Herald, Orion, Trieste, Victorio, Zefa Fino

lettuce

With the wide range of flavors, colors, and textures available to the lettuce grower, salads will never be the same again. Choose from lettuces that form tight heads, to looseleaf lettuces that can be cut whole or harvested a few leaves at a time as you need them.

Site & soil Lettuces prefer an open, sunny site, but they will tolerate light shade, and indeed benefit from it in warm weather. They grow in most garden soils as long as they are not waterlogged. Moisture-retentive soils are best, so choose soil that has had compost or manure added for a previous crop. Lettuces grow well under cover and in containers.

Sowing & planting If you have a greenhouse, cold frame, or hoop house, it is possible to sow and harvest lettuce in virtually any month of the year, although winter crops are the most difficult. Sow under cover in propagation trays in late winter, then harden off (see page 34) the young lettuces before planting in the garden. Lettuce generally takes 6–15 weeks from sowing to harvest.

Sow in the garden from spring onward, sowing a few seeds every two weeks to maintain a regular supply of fresh lettuce. Sow in drills ½ in. (1 cm) deep with 12 in. (30 cm) between rows. Thin the seedlings to 6–12 in. (15–30 cm) apart, depending on variety. If growing in blocks, space plants 6–14 in. (15–35 cm) apart.

Care Water lettuces well during periods of dry weather, so that their growth is not checked and they maintain their succulence. Weed regularly by hand or with a hoe, taking care not to dislodge or injure the plants.

Problems Check regularly for slugs and snails, which pose the biggest threat. In the unlikely event of any diseases striking, destroy the plants and start again elsewhere—it's not worth the effort to treat it.

Harvesting Pull or cut iceberg, Boston, and romaine lettuces as soon as they are big enough to harvest. If you have planned your sowing there should be a constant supply. Cut looseleaf varieties as whole heads, or simply remove as many leaves as you need at a time. The same plants will go on producing replacement leaves for some time, providing an economic use of space.

Storing Use lettuces as soon as they are harvested. They will last a short while in the vegetable compartment of the refrigerator but will soon lose their crisp freshness.

Good choices All Year Round, Bibb, Black Seeded Simpson, Buttercrunch, Catalogna Cerbiatta, Claremont, Corsair, Frillice, Great Lakes, Little Gem, Lobjoits Green, Lollo Bionda, Lollo Rossa, Matchless, Merlot, Oak Leaf, Parris Island Cos, Red Sails, Romulus, Ruby, Salad Bowl, Sangria, Tom Thumb, Webbs Wonderful, Winter Density

salad greens

From upland cress to miner's lettuce, arugula to sorrel, salad greens add a touch of the exotic to the salad bowl and a mix of flavors from mild to peppery. They are expensive to buy but ridiculously easy to grow, and you'll have the convenience of garden-fresh greens to hand whenever you want them.

Site & soil Most salad greens prefer a sunny, open site, but many will also tolerate light shade. They will grow in any reasonable garden soil. They also do well under cover, or even on a kitchen windowsill—most potting mixes are suitable for growing salad greens in containers.

Sowing & planting Sow just one type of salad green, or look out for seed mixtures that contain a selection of different plants. In warmer regions, salad greens can be sown at any time of year. They generally takes 3–10 weeks from sowing to harvest. For winter and early crops they are best grown under cover, but for the rest of the year they can be sown in the garden.

Sow thinly in drills ½ in. (1 cm) deep, with rows set 6–8 in. (15–20 cm) apart. There is usually no need to thin them. If growing in blocks, scatter the seed thinly, then rake it in, or sow in close drills.

Care Since most salad greens are small plants, it is important not to let them get swamped by weeds. Hand weed to avoid accidentally hoeing up the plants. Keep watered during dry weather, even during winter as the sun

can dry the soil rapidly when you are growing salad greens indoors or in a greenhouse.

Problems The most serious threat is likely to be from slugs. Flea beetles (see page 44) can be a nuisance with some of the crops, especially arugula: cover with insect-proof mesh or floating row cover. Keep a watch for birds—netting is the best way to keep them away from the plants. Generally, though, salad greens are fast growing and trouble free.

Harvesting Harvesting could not be simpler: just pick salad greens as you need them. Choose a few leaves from each type you grow, to make a varied salad bowl.

Storing It is best to pick salad greens as you need them—they do not store well. If necessary, they will keep for a day in the vegetable compartment of the refrigerator.

Good choices American cress, arugula, cress, lamb's lettuce, miner's lettuce, mitzuba, mustard greens, purslane, sorrel, watercress

endives

Endives are lettucelike plants that come in curly frisée varieties, or broad-leaved escaroles. They can be left with a slightly bitter twang, or they can be sweetened by blanching as they grow. These plants make a decorative and flavorsome addition to the salad bowl.

Site & soil Choose an open, sunny site if possible, although endives will tolerate light shade. They will grow in most soils, but a lighter soil is better for winter crops and waterlogged conditions should be avoided. If growing under cover, plant in the garden dirt or in containers filled with a good-quality potting soil.

Sowing & planting For early crops, sow in midspring under cover and grow the plants on under a hoop house or in a greenhouse. Transplant the young endives into the garden when conditions are warm enough, hardening them off before planting out (see page 34). Endives generally take 7–12 weeks from sowing to harvest.

Wait until conditions are warm enough to sow in the garden, usually by late spring in mild regions. Sow in drills ½ in. (1 cm) deep, with rows set 14 in. (35 cm) apart. When big enough, thin to about 12 in. (30 cm) intervals. If planting in blocks, set the plants 12 in. (30 cm) apart.

Care Keep well weeded, preferably by hand, and water regularly in dry weather. When the endives have reached maturity, they can be blanched to make them less bitter, by

covering the leaves for about ten days to exclude light. Wait until the leaves are dry, then cover the plant with a bucket for complete blanching or just cover the center of the plant with a plate.

Problems Slugs and snails can be a real nuisance. If you use slug pellets, make certain they do not lodge in the leaves of the plant. Aphids can be troublesome, especially to plants growing under cover. If an infestation occurs, remove by hand if you can.

Harvesting Harvest at any time when endives have reached maturity. If you blanch them, harvest soon after the ten days, as they will begin to deteriorate. Cut the head off rather than pulling out the whole plant, as you may get a second crop of leaves. If you don't need a whole head, simply remove a few of the leaves and leave the rest of the plant for cutting later.

Storing Use endives as soon as possible after cutting. They do not store well and can rarely be kept longer than a day with any degree of freshness.

Good choices Broad-leaved Batavian, Frisée Glory, Pancaliere, Pancalleri, Salad King, Tres Fin, Wallonne

chicory

Chicory produces tasty, bitter leaves, which can be used raw to perk up salads, or be braised and served hot. There are three types: radicchio for fall crops; Belgian or witloof chicory, which is forced for winter eating; and sugarloaf chicories, which have a milder flavor.

Site & soil Chicory will grow in full sun or light shade. The Belgian types need a deep soil; the others will grow in most garden soils as long as they are not too wet. The colorful, red radicchio can be grown in flower gardens, as they are quite decorative. Avoid very rich soil—soil amended for a previous crop is ideal.

Sowing & planting Chicory generally takes eight weeks or more from sowing to harvest. Belgian types are grown for forcing. Sow in the garden in midsummer in drills ½ in. (1 cm) deep. Thin plants to 8 in. (20 cm) apart, in rows 12 in. (30 cm) apart.

Sow radicchio outdoors in early summer, or in late summer for overwintering. Space as for Belgian chicory.

Sugarloaf types can be sown at any time of year under cover, or in the garden during the summer months. Space plants at 10 in. (25 cm) intervals.

Care Keep all chicories watered in dry weather. Belgian chicories need to be forced. Lift the roots in late fall and reduce them to 8 in. (20 cm); cut back the leaves to 2 in. (5 cm). Replant in large pots of moist potting soil with the

crowns just above the surface. Cover with a bucket to exclude all light and keep at about 55°F (13°C).

Problems Slugs are the most likely threat. Other than that, chicories are generally trouble free.

Harvesting Harvest sugarloaf and radicchio chicories as soon as they are big enough. Cut off the head rather than pulling up the whole plant, as the remaining stalk may sprout again. If you don't need a whole head, harvest just a few leaves and leave the rest for later.

Cut the blanched "chicons" of Belgian chicory after 3–4 weeks of forcing. Again, leave the stalk to resprout for a second crop.

Storing Chicory is best eaten as soon as it is harvested. It may last a day or so in a refrigerator but will lose its crispness.

Good choices Radicchio: Pallo Rosso, Red Verona, Rossano, Rosso di Chioggia,
Witloof: Totem
Sugarloaf: Pain de Sucre,

radishes

Radishes are quick and simple to grow just about anywhere, including in containers. Pull a few as a crunchy and nutritious nibble, or use to pep up your salads. They come in a wide range of colors, shapes, and flavors, and all taste better home grown than supermarket bought.

Site & soil Sow in an open, sunny site, or in light shade if the weather is warm. Radishes will grow in virtually any soil, but a light, moisture-retentive soil is ideal. If possible, choose soil enriched for a previous crop.

Sowing & planting Sow early crops under cover in the fall or late winter in their permanent places—they cannot be transplanted. Otherwise, sow in the garden from early spring onward. Radishes generally takes four weeks from sowing to harvest.

Sow just a few seeds at once: short rows at two-week intervals are better than infrequent, long rows. Save space by growing them between other slower-growing crops, such as parsnips or brassicas.

Sow the seed thinly in drills ½ in. (1 cm) deep with 6 in. (15 cm) between rows. Thin seedlings to 1 in. (2.5 cm) apart. If growing in blocks (see page 18), sprinkle the seed over the soil surface and lightly rake to cover it; thin the seedlings to about 3 in. (7 cm) apart, ensuring that the remaining seedlings are disturbed as little as possible. The large winter varieties need a little more space.

Care Do not allow the soil to dry out, as the radishes quickly become woody and very hot tasting. Keep the area weeded but be careful not to disturb the roots.

Problems Flea beetles (see page 44) may attack: cover the seedbed within insect-proof mesh or floating row cover, to prevent it. Slugs may also be a problem, especially with emerging seedlings.

Harvesting Harvest the radishes as soon as they are big enough. Be careful not to loosen adjacent plants as you pull them. Discard any that are obviously old or running to seed, as these will be woody and tough, and the flavor will be very hot.

Storing It is not possible to store radishes, so eat them as soon as they are harvested. They will keep for a day or so in the refrigerator, but will lose their crunchiness. Winter radishes can be left in the ground for longer, and should be covered with straw in frosty areas.

Good choices April Cross, Black Spanish Round, Cherry Belle, China Rose, Easter Egg, Flamboyant Sabrina, Fluo F1, French Breakfast, Mantanghong, Minowase, Munchen Bier, Pink Beauty, Rougette, Rudi, Sparkler, Summer Cross, White Icicle

tomatoes

Home-grown tomatoes, eaten while still warm from the sun, taste so much better than anything you can buy. Whether they are cherry, plum, or beefsteak tomatoes, red, yellow, green, or purple, choose varieties for their superior flavor and prepare to be amazed.

Site & soil Tomatoes need sunshine, so choose a warm, open site. They tolerate most soils, but prefer a well-drained, fertile soil. If planting in containers, use a good-quality potting soil. Avoid mixes that dry out rapidly, especially if you are growing your tomatoes in hanging baskets.

Sowing & planting Sow seeds one to a pot in late winter or spring, so the young plants are of a decent size for planting outdoors, as soon as the threat of frost has passed. Tomatoes generally takes eight weeks or more from sowing to harvest. A wide range of young tomato plants is available from garden centers and nurseries if you don't have anywhere warm and bright to raise the seedlings. After your last expected frost date, harden off the young plants (see page 34) and plant in the garden, 18 in. (45 cm) apart for indeterminate tomatoes and 24–36 in. (60–90 cm) apart for determinate varieties. Rows for both tomato types should be 36 in. (90 cm) apart. Plant at intervals of 18–24 in. (45–60cm) if planting in blocks (see page 18).

Care Indeterminate tomatoes need to be supported by stakes. Cut out any sideshoots as they appear to keep just

one central stem. Determinate varieties do not need supporting and the sideshoots are retained.

Water regularly and consistently once the fruit begins to swell. Fertilize plants with liquid 5–5–10 fertilizer—this is particularly important with container-grown plants, as the regular watering leaches nutrients from the soil.

Problems One of the worst problems is blight (see page 42). If you spot it, dig up and discard the plants to prevent it spreading. Intermittent watering can cause the fruit to split, so try to establish a routine and keep the soil just moist at all times.

Harvesting Pick the fruit as soon as it ripens. If frost threatens at the end of the season, pick the remaining green tomatoes and let them ripen indoors, or use them as green tomatoes in chutneys and other dishes.

Storing Tomatoes are always best when freshly picked, but they will keep in a bowl for a few days indoors. If you have a glut, cook and purée the excess and freeze for later use. At the end of the season, hang the plants upside down in a basement or garage and pick the fruit as it ripens, or ripen them on a windowsill in the kitchen.

Good choices Alicante, Better Boy, Big Boy, Black Prince, Brandy Wine, Celebrity, Early Girl, Gardener's Delight, Golden Cherry, Green Zebra, Husky Girl, Juliet, Marmande, Micro Tom, Moneymaker, Oregon Spring, Red Alert, San Mazano, Stupice, Sungold, Sweet Million, Tumbler, Tigrella, Viva Italia

eggplants

Eggplants are exciting vegetables with which to cook, being mainstays in Mediterranean, Middle Eastern, and Asian cuisines. Roast and purée them for patés and dips, bake in tomato sauce, or use in Indian curries. There is a wide range of colors and sizes from which to choose.

Site & soil Whether kept in containers or eventually planted in the open ground, eggplants are usually started under cover, in a greenhouse or on a sunny windowsill. When the temperature is above 68°F (20°C), move them outdoors to a warm, sunny site, preferably against a warm wall. They need deep, relatively rich soil with plenty of well-rotted organic matter. Container-grown plants require good-quality, rich potting soil.

Sowing & planting Soak the seed in warm water for a day before sowing. Sow seeds in cell packs or individual pots in late winter or early spring, preferably with gentle heat from an electric propagating unit. When large enough to plant outdoors and the threat of frost has passed, harden off the young plants (see page 34) and transplant them into the garden. Space them at intervals of 24–30 in. (60–75 cm), with 30–36 in. (75–90 cm) between rows. Leave 24–30 in. (60–75 cm) between plants if you are planting in blocks (see page 18). If continuing to be container-grown, transfer seedlings to 8 in. (20 cm) pots or grow bags. Eggplants generally take 16 weeks from sowing to harvest.

Care While tending them, watch out for the rather nasty spines, which can be painful. Keep the plants well watered and warm. Some varieties grow tall, so provide stakes for support if necessary. If you want larger fruit, restrict the plants to six fruit each. Apply a high-potassium fertilizer, such as liquid 5–5–10, once the fruit starts to swell.

Problems Eggplants are susceptible to whitefly, red spider mite, flea beetles, and aphids (see pages 42–4). Take any appropriate action if deemed necessary. Fungal diseases such as mildew may be a problem if there is not enough air circulating, so maintain good ventilation.

Harvesting Pick once the fruits are large enough. If they lose their shine or brown areas begin to form, they are past their best and should be discarded. Harvest by cutting the stalk where it joins the main stem, minding the prickles.

Storing Eggplants do not store very well but will keep for about a week in a cool place or in the refrigerator. If you have a glut, cut them up, fry in olive oil, and freeze for later use.

Good choices Black Beauty, Calliope, Fairy Tale F1, Gretel, Ichiban, Kermit F1, Moneymaker F1, Rosa Bianca

peppers and chili peppers

Easy, fun, and prolific, peppers are decorative plants for the patio and garden. Choose from red, orange, yellow, green, and purple varieties in a whole range of shapes, sizes, and flavors that may be sweet, mildly hot, or very hot. Use them in everything from Mediterranean to Oriental dishes.

Site & soil Peppers do best started under the cover of a greenhouse or hoop house, before being planted outdoors in a warm, sunny spot—against a warm wall is ideal—in fertile, well-drained soil. Use a good, all-purpose potting soil in containers.

Sowing & planting There is a huge range of seed on offer for peppers, and a good range of young plants in garden centers in late spring. Peppers generally takes 20 weeks from sowing to harvest.

Sow the seed under cover in individual pots or cell packs in mid- to late spring. Avoid sowing earlier unless you have a heated greenhouse. When large enough, transfer the young plants to larger pots or grow bags. If you are planting them outdoors, wait until all risk of frost is over and the temperature is above 59°F (15°C), then harden off the young plants (see page 34) and transplant them into the garden. Space the plants at intervals of 12–18 in. (30–45 cm), with rows 24–36 in. (60–90 cm) apart.

Care The temperature must not drop below 59°F (15°C), although 70–86°F (21–30°C) is best. The soil will dry out

rapidly at these temperatures, so keep an eye on plants, as they may need watering several times a day. As fruit begins to develop, fertilize with a high-potassium fertilizer, such as liquid 5–5–10.

Problems If peppers are growing in a greenhouse, whitefly, red spider mite, and aphids can be troublesome (see pages 42–4). Take action only if they become a serious problem. Keep the plants well ventilated, to prevent fungal diseases such as mildew.

Harvesting Harvest as soon as the fruit is big enough. Chili peppers get hotter the longer they are grown, so harvest as you like them. Sweet peppers change color as they age—green, red, yellow—and they also become sweeter. Again, harvest as you like them.

Storing Peppers are best eaten soon after picking, although they will keep for a few days in a cool place. If you have a glut, they freeze well. At the end of the season, hang the plants upside down in a frost-free but cool area, and pick as required. Hot peppers can be dried and stored in an airtight jar.

Best choices Peppers: Ace F1, Bianca, Blushing Beauty, California Wonder, Carmen, Giant Marconi, Gourmet, Gypsy F1, Large Sweet Cherry, Redskin, Sunray, Sweet Banana, Sweet Chocolate, Sweet Pimento
Chili peppers: Anaheim, Apache F1, Big Sun, Cayenne, Demon Red, Etna, Holy Mole, Hungarian Hot Wax, Jalapeño, Mariachi, Thai Hot

cucumber

Home-grown cucumbers are far superior in both taste
and texture to watery supermarket fare. Cucumbers range
from large slicing cucumbers, with their smooth or warty
skins, to small, gherkin types, which are suitable for pickling
or eating raw, in salads.

Site & soil For an early crop, start cucumbers under cover,
in containers, hoop houses, or in a greenhouse. Any good-
quality potting mix will do. Grow maincrops in an open,
sunny site in the garden, although cucumber plants will
tolerate a little shade especially during a hot summer. They
need a fertile, friable, free-draining soil.

Sowing & planting Don't start cucumbers too early: the
best time for sowing an early crop is four weeks before
your last expected frost date. Cucumbers generally take
12 weeks from sowing to harvest. Sow seeds in cell packs
or individual pots. Put two seeds in each pot, placing the
seeds on their sides so they rest in the soil on one edge. If
both germinate, remove one seedling as soon as possible.
As soon as they are big enough and all risk of frost has
passed, harden off the young plants (see page 34) and
plant them in the garden.

  For maincrop cucumbers, sow direct in the garden in drills
½ in. (1 cm) deep, with rows 24–30 in. (60–75 cm) apart.
Use similar distances if planting in blocks (see page 18).
Vining cucumbers can also be allowed to sprawl, in which
case they may need 3–4 ft. (90–120 cm) between plants.

Care Vining varieties need a support over which to grow—stakes, strings, or netting are the most usual. Bush varieties do not require this. Pinch back the growing tip when the plant reaches the top of the support or has covered enough ground. Keep well watered, especially in hot weather.

Problems Red spider mite, whitefly, aphids, and slugs can can be a nuisance (see pages 42–4).

Harvesting Cut the cucumbers when they are big enough, removing them with a small length of stalk still attached. Once fully grown, do not leave on the plant too long, or they will turn yellow.

Storing Cucumbers are best eaten straight from the plant. They will keep for a few days in a cool place but not much longer. Gherkins can be eaten fresh or pickled.

Good choices Albi, Birgit F1, Burpee Pickler, Burpless Tasty Green, Bush Champion, Bush Champion F1, Carmen F1, Diamant, Diva, Fanfare, Futura F1, Lemon, Long White, Marketmore F1, Pickalot, Salad Bush, Saladin F1, Straight Eight, Suyo Long, Sweet Success

zucchini

Zucchini are a summer staple and hugely versatile in the kitchen. Even one plant will produce a good crop of delicious, green or yellow fruits that can be cylindrical or spherical. Both zucchini and and other summer squash are easy and prolific plants.

Site & soil Choose an open, sunny site sheltered from strong winds or the large leaves will get torn. Zucchini will grow in any good garden soil, preferably one rich in humus (see page 12), so add plenty of well-rotted compost or animal manure. Some gardeners grow them in a pocket of soil in an old compost pile.

Sowing & planting Either sow seed under cover in early spring, or outdoors in late spring. Don't sow too early: plant out young plants grown under cover, or germinate seed in the garden, just after the last threat of frost. Zucchini generally take eight weeks from sowing to harvest.

If raising young plants under cover, sow two seeds in each cell pack or individual pot with the seeds lying on their edges. Remove the weaker seedling if they both germinate. Harden off plants (see page 34) before planting outdoors.

To sow outdoors, sow two seeds 3 ft. (1 m) apart for bush varieties and up to 6 ft. (2 m) apart for trailing ones. Use similar spacings if you are block planting (see page 18).

Care Keep plants well watered, especially when they are establishing themselves. Train trailing varieties up strong

supports or spread the foliage out evenly over the ground. Anchor long stems in more windy sites.

Problems Slugs are among the worst enemies of zucchini, which are most vulnerable when the plants have just germinated or been planted out. Various viruses (see page 44) can also strike—remove badly affected plants.

Harvesting Pick the zucchini as they become big enough. The smaller they are, the better flavor and texture they have, but if the crop is limited allow them to grow slightly bigger. Remove any that become too large to encourage more smaller fruits to grow.

Storing Zucchini will keep for a few days in the refrigerator, but are best eaten as soon as possible after picking. If you have a glut, slice and fry them in a little oil and freeze them for soups, sauces, and casseroles.

Good choices All Green Bush, Black Beauty, Burpee's Golden, Eight Ball, Gold Rush F1, Magda, Raven, Spineless Beauty

pumpkins and squashes

Well known for their associations with Halloween, pumpkins also make a delicious ingredient in the kitchen. Winter squashes are very similar to pumpkins and can be treated the same. Summer squashes are cultivated in the same way as zucchini (see pages 204–7).

Site & soil Pumpkins and winter squashes prefer an open, sunny site, although they will tolerate some shade. They like a deep soil, rich in organic matter (see page 12), so add plenty of well-rotted compost or manure. For the biggest pumpkins, grow the plants in a pocket of soil on an old manure or compost pile.

Sowing & planting If you are growing them to eat, rather than making lanterns or entering giant pumpkin competitions, it is best to choose a small pumpkin variety, or grow winter squashes instead. Young plants are available from garden centers, but these are likely to be the large-fruiting varieties. Pumpkins and squashes generally take 12 weeks from sowing to harvest.

Sow the seed under cover so the young plants will be ready to plant in the garden as soon as the risk of frost is over. Set the seeds on their sides in individual pots and cover with potting soil. Grow on under cover, then harden off (see page 34), before planting outdoors. Planting distances vary so check on the packet for the recommended one for your variety: bush varieties tend to need 2–3 ft. (60–100 cm), while trailing ones need up to twice that distance.

Care Keep the area well weeded, but avoid loosening the plant while doing so. Water well while the plants are becoming established. Trailing varieties can be trained up supports or left to trail along the ground; peg stems down in windy areas, if necessary.

Problems Slugs are a nuisance, especially when the plants are first planted in the garden or when the seedlings first emerge if sown *in situ*. Later they will also eat into the fruits. Mildew (see pages 42–4) can also be a problem—ensure there is plenty of air circulating and ignore all but very serious cases.

Harvesting Pick as soon as the fruits become large enough. Cut the fruits from the main stem, leaving a piece of stalk on each pumpkin or squash. If you intend to store the fruits, leave them on the plants as long as possible.

Storing Pumpkins and winter squashes will keep for several months, depending on the variety. Leave on the plants until just before the first predicted frost, then cut and store in a dry, cool, airy place which is free from frost.

Good choices Pumpkins: Aladdin F1, Baby Bear, Dill's Atlantic Giant, Lumina, Mars F1, Small Sugar Spellbound F1
Winter squashes: Blue Hubbard, Butternut, Festival F1, Honey Bear, Orange Dawn, Sweet Dumpling, Turk's Turban
Summer squashes: Bush Baby, Cristoforo, Early Golden Crookneck, Long Green Bush, Peter Pan, Scallopini Mix, Sunburst F1, Zephyr F1

spinach

Spinach is packed with vitamins A and C, and is perfect for stir-fries, casseroles, soups, and raw in delicious salads. Pick the leaves while young and tender if you are eating them raw, or allow them to mature for cooked dishes. Spinach is easy to grow, as long as the weather is not too hot.

Site & soil Spinach is one of the few crops that grows happily in light shade, indeed in hot, summer weather this is the best place for it, as it has a tendency to bolt if too hot. Choose an open, airy site or grow fall sowings under cover. Spinach will tolerate most soils, but does best on a plot enriched for a previous crop.

Sowing & planting In many regions, sow from late winter or early spring for an early crop. In all areas, then sow a few seeds at two-week intervals until early fall, to get a continuous crop. Spinach generally takes five weeks from sowing to harvest.

Sow the seed in drills ½ in. (1 cm) deep, with 12 in. (30 cm) between rows. Thin the seedlings when big enough, to about 6 in. (15 cm) apart. Small-leaf varieties can be thinned to about 4 in. (10 cm). To reduce the amount of thinning, you can spot sow (see page 34). If you are growing in blocks (see page 18), space plants about 6 in. (15 cm) apart.

Care Spinach is easy to care for, particularly as it is a fast-growing crop. Keep the area well weeded, particularly in the

early stages of its growth. Water if necessary, to keep the spinach growing steadily. This is important in warm weather.

Problems Spinach is not susceptible to many pests and diseases. Occasionally it may suffer from mildew (see pages 42–4) in a confined area, but good ventilation will help prevent this. The only other problem is bolting (see page 212) about which little can be done once it happens. To prevent it, keep plants growing steadily by watering well and plant later crops in light shade.

Harvesting Start to pick the leaves as soon as they are large enough, taking just a few leaves from each plant. If you need the whole plant, cut above the main stalk and it may reshoot with more leaves. Keep picking until the plants begin to bolt. If you have sown at two-week intervals, there should be a steady supply.

Storing Spinach does not store when fresh and should be used as soon as it is picked. It will, however, freeze well if you wilt the leaves first.

Good choices 7-Green, Bloomsdale Longstanding, Bordeaux F1, Giant Winter, Indian Summer, Rembrandt, Samish F1, Skookum, Space, Spargo, Tyee

new zealand spinach

This easy-going leaf vegetable is a great substitute for spinach in the kitchen and is much simpler to grow as it has no tendency to bolt (see page 212). It also has a long season of production, so you could be picking fresh and nutritious leaves year-round.

Site & soil New Zealand spinach plants tolerate a wide range of conditions and soils, including hot, dry ones, making it very easy to accommodate in the garden.

Sowing & planting Sow in the garden from mid- to late spring in drill ¾ in. (2 cm) deep, with rows set about 16 in. (40 cm) apart. Thin seedlings to about 18 in (45 cm) apart. Spot sow (see page 34) if preferred, to avoid a lot of thinning. If planting in blocks (see page 18), plant at the same distance. New Zealand spinach generally takes eight weeks from sowing to harvest.

Care New Zealand spinach tends to ramble across the soil and could become entangled in weeds, making harvesting difficult, so keep the area well weeded. Plants will tolerate drought conditions.

Problems Apart from the usual nuisance of slugs attacking young or emerging plants, New Zealand spinach is generally trouble free.

Harvesting Start to pick individual leaves as soon as the first leaves are big enough. They will go on producing for a long period. If the plants begin to look tired, cut off all leaves and let a new crop grow. You can pick and eat the shoot tips of New Zealand spinach as well as the leaves.

Storing The leaves wilt soon after picking, so use as fresh as possible. It will freeze quite well.

Good choices New Zealand spinach is rarely sold as anything other than its name.

swiss chard

Whether it is smooth or crinkly, white, pink, yellow, purple, or rainbow colors, swiss chard is a feast for the eyes as well as the stomach. The freshly picked leaves of this highly decorative plant have a crispness and flavor that tired leaves from the shops can never achieve.

Site & soil Swiss chard is a tolerant plant that grows in sun or shade, and will happily survive in windy sites. It will grow in most garden soils and in deep containers. If you are growing it in the flower garden, position it so the evening sun illuminates the colors in the leaves.

Sowing & planting Sow maincrops of Swiss chard direct in the garden. It is important to sow thinly as each "seed" is in fact a cluster of several seeds. Late-summer sowings will provide winter crops, which can be grown either indoors or outdoors, although the former will produce better leaves. Swiss chard generally takes eight weeks from sowing to harvest.

Sow in drills ¾ in. (2 cm) deep, with rows set 18 in. (45 cm) apart. You need to thin the emerging seedlings to about 9 in. (23 cm) apart, so it is best to spot sow (see page 34) at roughly these intervals. If you are planting Swiss chard in blocks (see page 18), space plants 12 in. (30 cm) apart.

Care Swiss chard needs little maintenance considering the length of its season. Water in dry weather to keep it

growing well. For outdoors winter crops, the quality of the leaves can be improved by covering with a hoop house or floating row cover.

Problems This is a trouble-free crop that rarely needs any attention. It can suffer from beet leaf spot, a mild fungal disease that shows as round spots on the leaves, with a pale center and purple edge. This problem is not worth worrying about as the damage rarely affects the quality of the vegetable so no remedy is usually required. Beet leaf miners can also be a minor irritant. The white larvae make large, brown patches on the leaves. If you come across any, just squeeze the larvae between your fingers.

Harvesting You can start cutting the Swiss chard leaves as soon as they are big enough, but allow the plant to retain some so that it has the energy to grow to full size. If, as the season progresses, the leaves become large and rather coarse, cut all the foliage off and allow the plant to regenerate.

Storing Swiss chard leaves soon begin to wilt after picking, so they are best used straight from the plant. However, they can be frozen successfully.

Good choices Bright Lights, Bright Yellow, Charlotte, Fordhook Giant, Lucullus, Rhubarb Chard

seakale

Seakale is a culinary treat. The stems are steamed like asparagus, while the leaves are used as spring greens. The plant crops well for about six years, and it is an invaluable addition to potagers (see page 24) for its silvery-gray foliage and masses of white flowers.

Site & soil In the wild, seakale grows on the beach, so it likes a sunny, open site. The soil should be sandy and free draining, but you should add a certain amount of well-rotted organic material (see page 12). Prepare the site well, as the plant will be there for a number of years.

Sowing & planting Seakale can be sown from seed or planted as "thongs" (pieces of root). The seed has a very hard case, so scratch the surface with sandpaper before sowing. Sow in pots or in the open ground in spring, and move to their final places when they are big enough. Seakale generally takes two years from sowing to harvest, while thongs take one year from planting to harvest.

You can either buy thongs or take them as root cuttings from a three-year-old plant in early winter. Stand the pieces of root upright in damp sand in a cool place. Plant out in midspring, once buds have formed on the top of each, spacing the plants 24 in. (60 cm) apart.

Care Not a great deal of attention is required, but keep the area weeded, as the plants do not like to be overgrown. Fertilize plants every year after harvesting (see page 36)

by mulching the soil with well-rotten compost and forking in a little bonemeal or seaweed meal.

Problems Seakale is generally trouble free. Slugs can be a nuisance and eat enough of the emerging foliage to kill the plant; reduce their numbers, using whichever method of control you prefer.

Harvesting In late winter or early spring, cover the plants with a bucket to exclude all light, then cover with straw or bubble wrap to keep the plants a little warmer. The resulting blanched stems can be cut once they are big enough. Continue cutting off the stems until late spring, then leave the plant to recover.

Storing Seakale does not keep well, so it should be used as soon as it is harvested.

Good choices This plant is normally simply sold as seakale or *Crambe maritima*

rhubarb

The first, delicate pink rhubarb stems of the season are a long-awaited luxury for vegetable gardeners everywhere. Rhubarb is an easy and prolific plant that goes on producing for many years. The distinctive flavor of its handsome, red stems complements both sweet and savory dishes.

Site & soil Rhubarb will grow in sun or light shade. It will tolerate a windy site, but benefits from some protection. It will happily grow on most soils, except waterlogged ones, but does best in a deep, fertile soil. Prepare the bed well before planting by digging in plenty of well-rotted organic material (see page 12).

Sowing & planting It is possible to grow rhubarb from seed but the results are variable, so it is better to grow from root cuttings, called "sets." Plant into ground that was prepared six months before so all perennial weeds have been removed. Plant in mid- to late fall, or in late winter to early spring, whenever the weather and soil are suitable. The latter period is better for cold or wet areas. Rhubarb generally takes 12 months from planting to harvest.

Plant with the crown just below the soil surface. One clump is often enough, but, if you are planting more, space them 3 ft. (1 m) apart.

Care Keep the area free from perennial weeds, which will be difficult to eradicate, once established. Remove the flower stalks as soon as they appear on the plant. Mulch

each fall with well-rotted organic material (see page 38) and cut away the dead leaves to let the frost get to the crown.

Problems Rhubarb should give years of trouble-free service. On rare occasions, it may get a viral infection (see page 44). If this happens, dig up the plant and discard it. Don't replant on the same site—choose a new site some distance away.

Harvesting In its second year, start to pull the stems, not cut them, as they appear in spring, leaving about half of them on the plant. Stop harvesting in midsummer, to give time for the plant to regenerate. Some varieties can be forced after the first few frosts to encourage them to produce tender early stems. Do this by covering the plant with a deep bucket or garbage can, to exclude all light, then cover the bucket with straw to keep the plant a little warmer. You should get a crop around three weeks early.

Storing Rhubarb does not store well fresh, but it can be frozen once cooked.

Good choices Canada Red, Strawberry, Valentine, Victoria

corn

Home-grown sweet corn is far superior to anything you can buy—the sugars start to convert to starch after picking, so the fresher it is, the sweeter it is. Barbecue the cobs whole straight after picking. Choose "supersweet" cultivars for flavor, or quick-maturing varieties for cooler climates.

Site & soil Corn likes a sunny, open site. Avoid very windy places, although corn *en masse* does not generally suffer wind damage. It will grow on most soils as long as they are not too dry nor too wet. A free-draining, moderately fertile soil is best. Corn can be grown under cover—useful in areas where the soil takes a long time to warm up in spring.

Sowing & planting Sow corn under cover in cell packs or individual pots in midspring, or outdoors in the open garden in early summer. Don't sow too early—all risk of frost must be over before plants are planted outdoors, and the soil should be at 61°F (16°C) for outdoor sowing or planting. Cover the soil with landscape fabric to warm it up. Corn generally takes 12 weeks from sowing to harvest.

To aid pollination, it is important to grow corn in blocks rather than rows. If spot sowing (see page 34), set plants at 12–14 in. (30–35 cm) intervals.

Care Keep well weeded, preferably by hand as corn plants resent root disturbance. In windy areas it may be necessary to protect against the wind or support the plants—some gardeners hill the stems slightly as the plant grows, to

develop more supporting roots. Water well as the cobs begin to fill out.

Problems Generally corn is trouble free. Slugs can attack young plants, so keep them at bay. Mice and birds can steal the sown seed or the ripening cobs. Netting is about the only way to prevent this. Small areas of plants will suffer more than large ones.

Harvesting When the silk tassels turn brown, the corn is ripe and can be cut from the plant just below the cob.

Storing There is no doubt that sweet corn tastes best when cooked straight after picking, but it will keep a few days in the refrigerator. It also freezes well.

Good choices Country Gentleman, Early Sunglow, Extra Tender & Sweet, Golden Bantam, Indian Summer F1, Iochief, Kandy Korn, Northern Extra Sweet, Silver Queen